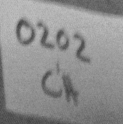

DISCOVER

IRONSTONE
Vineyards

DISCOVER
IRONSTONE
Vineyards

HIDDEN TREASURES *from*
CALIFORNIA'S GOLD COUNTRY

RECIPES BY
EXECUTIVE CHEF
DAN LEWIS

PHOTOGRAPHY BY
TIM TURNER

EDITED BY
JUDI CARLE AND **LORI KAUTZ**

Table *of* Contents

APPETIZERS

SOUPS & SALADS

SOUPS & SALADS *continued*

ENTRÉES

DESSERTS

Introduction

WELCOME TO IRONSTONE VINEYARDS, a winery as unique as any single gold nugget. Renowned for world-class quality wines and unparalleled gracious hospitality, we are excited to present a sampling of our culinary expertise.

Under the direction of Executive Chef Dan Lewis, the culinary staff at Ironstone Vineyards provides an outstanding fine-dining experience. From intimate wine-maker dinners to elegant weddings, gourmet barbeques, concert picnics, seasonal Sunday brunches, and a daily gourmet deli, the recipes must be flexible for every occasion. To heighten the gastronomic experience, each ingredient is chosen to meld impeccably with the sensorial components in Ironstone wines.

Chef Dan enjoys occasionally departing from the "standard" rules of food and wine pairing by enhancing distinctive flavors and utilizing unique ingredients. Since many of the parties held at Ironstone Vineyards are for larger groups, the food cannot be excessively complicated to prepare. At the same time, the entire experience must be presented attractively and the quality and flavors must be exceptional.

The recipes presented in this book follow Chef Dan's basic philosophy—"Really Simple, Really Impressive, and, most important, Really Good!"

Ironstone Vineyards, founded in 1989 by John and Gail Kautz, is owned and operated by the Kautz family. Their passion for promoting agri-tourism became the heart of developing the winery as a tourist destination. The vineyards and winery are located in the Sierra Foothills of Calaveras County, California, one mile from the historic Gold Rush town of Murphys.

We invite you to discover the majestic charm of Ironstone Vineyards. As you meander down a country road, past an old barn and green rolling pastures, you'll find the vineyards nestled among oaks and pines.

Stephen Kautz enjoys a little solitude in tractor rumble while eradicating some weeds.

Roses abound along a fence line to open pasture for livestock.

Round the bend and enter the main gates, passing under an oar cart trestlework built upon natural stone. The seven-story winery and visitor center complex side steps down a solid rock mountain while nestled in native flora. As you approach the tasting room, you're greeted by barrels of seasonal flowers along the walkway. Inside you're invited to belly up to the bar and sample Ironstone Vineyards' award winning wines. The historic bar was built in 1907 by the New Brunswick Bowling Ball Company and has sailed around Cape Horn to finally find its home. Drop down a level and you'll find the educational culinary center, which opens into the Grand Music Room where you can listen to the 1200 pipe, 1927 Robert Morton Theatre Organ, which was originally housed at the Alhambra Theatre in Sacramento. Explore the Galleries and California's Gold Mining Museum. Relax with a casual stroll through the twelve acres

Working water wheel constructed on site using recycled timbers and an original center hub from the late 1800's.

ABOVE: Hundreds of visitors have had their photo taken with this fellow. Despite his labors, he's always there to greet you at the entrance gazebo. BELOW: Lawns and gardens surround the facility creating an unobtrusive atmosphere.

of landscaped gardens and perhaps you'll come across the secluded pathway along a hidden creek. You'll also find a replicated miner's shack, gold mine and working water wheel with gold stamp mill. There is something for every family member to discover that is sure to leave a lasting impression.

Let this cookbook be your guide to creating impressive meals for friends and family. They will think you were a slave to the kitchen for hours, but you can just smile and take credit for the fabulous feast. As you become familiar with the recipes and creative use of ingredients, you will see that many can be easily incorporated into your everyday meals.

The Kautz Family

The Kautz family has traced their German farming heritage back some five hundred years. The original families traveled from the Bavarian Alps to the Volga River region of Russia in the late 1700s and then to the United States in the late 1800s. John Kautz's parents finally met and were married in Nebraska, only to discover that they had been born in villages less than five miles apart. They traveled to a German settlement in Lodi, California, searching for work in 1923.

John lived a typical family farm life while growing up. The family grew and canned vegetables, and they raised dairy cows for fresh milk, cream, and butter. In 1941 John's father, Fred, was able to purchase a primary piece of farmland, a total of thirty-eight acres. John took over the family farm at the young age of twenty-two, and with hard work, vision and foresight, fortune shined. In 1958 he married his life partner, Gail Kramer.

Gail is a third-generation Californian, raised in Oakland, but Murphys was her home away from home as she grew up.

When Gail's father, Bauer Kramer, returned from World War II he resumed his law practice in Oakland, but desired to fulfill his passion for ranching. Gail's grandfather, John Burgess, was working as a mining engineer at the Melones and Carson Hill mines and found the property for her father in the quaint town of Murphys. On this ranch land that her father purchased in 1948, she cultivated her adventurous spirit and love of animals, especially horses. Gail's grandfather also instilled in her a passionate respect for California's history.

Together, John and Gail raised tomatoes, bell peppers, cherries, apples, and a family. In 1965, John was named the Outstanding Young Farmer of the Nation and later joined the board of the Top Farmers of America, setting up the first agri-tourism program. This enabled John and Gail to travel domestically and abroad with fellow Top Farmers, sharing knowledge from around the world. It was through these travels that John became inspired to plant wine grapes.

John Kautz Farms vigorously began planting Bordeaux varieties of wine grapes in 1968 and in the mid-1970s was the first to plant Chardonnay in Lodi. The 105-acre crop was contracted to Napa area wineries. "Planting Chardonnay was a very valuable decision," said John. "From there it was evident that the premium wine grape industry was our family's clear path."

John and Gail were able to purchase her family's property, and the dream to create a winery and vineyards in Murphys was born. More than just a winery, they envisioned a destination for experiencing fine wines and exceptional foods presented with gracious hospitality. The facility had to be state-of-the-art while complementing the notably outstanding mining and ranching heritage of the local area.

It all began when ten thousand square feet of caves were hand blasted using techniques developed by the gold miners 150 years earlier. A small rock mountain was sculpted to support this seven-story multi-purpose winery and entertainment facility, now viewed as one of California's most appealing visitor attractions.

John and Gail Kautz are delighted as their children continue the family business. Today, the farms encompass more than five thousand acres of wine grapes throughout the Lodi appellation and Sierra Foothills regions. With the purchase of Bear Creek Winery in Lodi, an expansive bulk wine facility, the Kautz family's winemaking

Gail and John Kautz

capacity became one of the top twenty-five in California.

Each family member oversees major segments within the operation. Oldest son Stephen Kautz is president of Ironstone Vineyards, managing wine sales and the winery facility. Kurt is the controller for the farming operation and oversees Bear Creek Winery, and Jack is involved in wine sales and property development. Daughter Joan Kautz-Meier is the vice-president of international operations. Not just the immediate family, but other family members, including cousins, nieces, and nephews are also involved in the daily farming, vineyard, and winery operations.

No matter how busy family members are each day, it has always been a Kautz tradition to gather around the dinner table to enjoy the meal, appreciate the simple things in life, and toast to family, good wine, good food, and good friends.

That precious little yellow metal that drives men crazy!

—MARK TWAIN

Gold!

The cries of gold brought Italians, Germans, Chinese, Irish, French, Spanish and many others. Fortune seekers from around the world came to California during the great Gold Rush in the mid-1800s. For the first time in history, opportunists from just about every ethnic background found themselves gathered together in one place.

In this unsettled territory, familiar food supplies were limited or unobtainable. The settlers used what was available regionally and what they had brought from their homelands. These sundries of provisions led to the creation of a totally new cuisine, a fusion as diverse and imaginative as the immigrants themselves.

Many pioneers of the California Gold Rush recognized the soils and climate of the Mother Lode were similar to those of their homelands. These miners discovered an entirely new gold in wine grapes. By 1870 there were over a hundred operating wineries in the Sierra Foothills.

Just as the Gold Rush opened the door for explorers to discover what became California, this book will open your palate to discover the outstanding culinary creations of Ironstone's Executive Chef Dan Lewis.

Cooking, like winemaking, is a marriage of flavors. You can give the same dessert recipe to five different friends, and the end product would be five different desserts. It is the people that create the cuisine, and with this in mind, we invite you to take the easy-to-prepare recipes and ideas in this book to discover your own gold mine of flavors and explore new territories in the art of blending of food and wine.

OPPOSITE: The largest crystalline leaf gold specimen in the world at 44 pounds is a Crown Jewel of the Sierras. Discovered just 20 miles away, it is on permanent display in Ironstone Vineyards Museum.

Executive Chef Dan Lewis

First and foremost, I thank God for everything He has given me, including the modest measure of talent that has allowed me to complete this project, the Kautz family for the opportunities they have given me, and my family for their patience, support, and love.

My culinary interests were sparked as a boy growing up in Monterey. I have fond memories of digging clams in the surf, catching Dungeness crabs on the wharf, squid fishing in the middle of the night, and early morning trout fishing in Big Sur—enjoying the catch that same morning at breakfast. The bounty from neighborhood vegetable gardens, the fruit trees in my backyard, and my grandfather's orchard all contributed to my early culinary makeup.

At that time I didn't know anything about cooking all of these wonderful things. That was left to my mother, who was and is a very good cook. But, I loved to eat them and developed a taste for the best and freshest ingredients to go along with the four things I think you need to be a good cook: heart, soul, salt, and pepper.

At the age of fourteen I got my first restaurant job on Fisherman's Wharf in Monterey. I continued my career in the kitchen as a dishwasher at Del Monte Lodge in Pebble Beach, where I met Chef Michel Marcais, one of only a handful of true master chefs in the United States at the time. After a year of hard work, I was promoted to pot washer. I know this doesn't sound like much, but the pot sink was at the end of the cooks' line, and I got to put cheese on the onion soup—my first professional cooking duty.

When I worked my way to dinner line cook at the lodge, Chef Michel moved to New Orleans and offered me a position in the kitchen of the Royal Sonesta, a five-hundred-room four-star hotel on Bourbon

Street. Chef Michel taught me to do things right. In my four-year tenure there, I learned to cook with my heart and began to develop my own style.

Upon moving back to California, my first serious exposure to food and wine pairing came while working at Souverain Winery in Sonoma County. I started to think of wine as more of a food or ingredient rather than just a beverage—an integral part of the dining experience.

The following spring I found myself working as sous chef at the Au Relais, a French country restaurant in Sonoma. The greatest thing happened in the kitchen there. I met my wife-to-be, Monica. We worked side by side doing great food. Those were wonderful times, though I had a hard time keeping my mind on my work.

At this point in my career, I felt it was important to learn as much as I could from as many as possible. When my learning curve started to level off at one job, I would look for new challenges in another kitchen—always moving up the culinary ladder, always learning. This brought me to the Sonoma Mission Inn as sous chef.

This was an exciting time to be cooking in California wine country because what became known as California cuisine was just taking off, and we embraced it at the Mission Inn. We had farmers, foragers, and dairymen coming to the back door daily.

Monica, now my wife, had an opportunity to open a bakery on Maui with a former

employer, and so in Hawaii, I was able to expand my culinary repertoire to include Pacific Rim and some Asian cuisine.

Fate brought us back to Monterey (well, if you call phoning an old chef buddy for a job "fate"), and I became sous chef at the

Sardine Factory on Cannery Row. Chef Bert Cutino offered me my first official chef's job at the Rogue on Fisherman's Wharf. I had come full circle; I was back at the wharf.

Fresh seafood made up the bulk of the menu. I would look out the window and see the fishing boats down at the end of the pier unloading, call the fishmonger to see what they had brought in, and ten minutes later here he came on his little forklift with my fish for the night. It doesn't get any better than that.

Monica and I moved back to Sonoma (another circle) and here my first daughter, Brianna, was born. The next challenge in my culinary journey came as executive chef of All Season's Party Productions, a full-service catering company in Marin County. While catering for parties with 40 to 2,500 people, we also handled the food service at Tiburon's Corinthian Yacht Club on San Francisco Bay. I was also stand-in chef for a couple of months at George Lucas's Skywalker Ranch. Skywalker Ranch by day, the Yacht Club by night—that was interesting.

We moved to Washington for family reasons, and I found a chef's job at the Ridpath Hotel. My family had now grown to four with the birth of my second daughter, Haley. Then, there is the story of "Discovering Ironstone."

One day as I walked through one of the hotel's restaurants, I saw a little wine tasting in the corner and invited myself (chefs can do that). Ironstone's regional representative, was pitching Ironstone wines to our fine-dining restaurant manager, and I said to him jokingly, "Why don't you get me a job as the chef for the winery?" I didn't even know if Ironstone had any kind of food service. He said he thought they were looking for a chef, and five days later I came to Murphys for an interview. I knew I would like it here—not only Ironstone, but Murphys and the entire Sierra Foothills area. Stephen Kautz and I worked out an agreement, and I started working for Ironstone in June of 1998.

When I'm right, I'm right. We all fell in love with the area and the Murphys community. I couldn't ask for a better work environment. Monica makes all of the wedding cakes and helps with the pastries. So, I get to do what I love with the one that I love.

I have an herb garden and a large variety of edible flowers throughout the winery. I am always in trouble with the grounds keeping staff for stealing flowers. With the vineyard, the beautiful gardens, the great wines, and the freedom to be as creative as I want. I am living large.

Eat Well
Drink Wine
Live Large

—EXECUTIVE CHEF DAN LEWIS

Food *and* Wine Pairing

The art of pairing wine and food should be approached with innovation and passion, keeping in mind that there are many levels of success in the marriage. In a good food and wine pairing, the food and wine get along or are happy together. In a great pairing, they enhance and uplift each other, yet both are successful matches.

I have suggested a wine varietal to complement the unique flavor components of each dish. However, I encourage you to experiment! There are more food and wine choices than ever before. The standard rules may not necessarily apply—don't be afraid to break the "rules," because in the end it's about what combinations you enjoy. (The president of Ironstone will tell you that I practice what I preach.)

When you are cooking, consider building flavors with bridge ingredients that will bring your food and wine tastes together. Trial and error is the best method I have found for pairing. Do not be afraid to try new things. But, most importantly, have fun and enjoy the process.

The Seven Deadly Sins or Ugly Sisters

The following food components present a challenge in food and wine pairing, but can be tweaked so they are happy with wine.

ASPARAGUS—A tough one, but not impossible. Penne with Asparagus and Lemon Cream is a good example of how bridge ingredients help a tough ingredient work wonderfully with Chardonnay. The lemon peel enhances the citrus flavors of the Chardonnay while balancing the flavors of the asparagus.

ARTICHOKE—Artichokes have an acid in them that makes things taste sweet. So, the best wines to try would be drier with some acid, such as Sauvignon Blanc.

CHILES—The heat in chiles, can be a problem. I like hot and spicy food, but when it's more than just mildly hot, the heat from the peppers will make oaky or tannic wines taste more tannic. It also brings the alcohol taste way up, making your wine taste hot. Fruity off-dry Symphony, Gewurztraminer, whites, and soft (low-tannin) fruit reds such as Pinot Noir, Zinfandel (under 13.5 percent alcohol), White Zinfandel, and, rose´ are your best choices here.

EGGS—I have not found anything that really works well with eggs. If you really want to pair these, try a quiche or Basque frittata with a fruity Chardonnay. Keep your "bridge ingredients" in mind and work with them.

VINEGAR—Most vinegars on their own are an enemy to wine, but in vinaigrettes for salads and adding small amounts to sauces, you can make some nice pairings. Adding a pinch of sugar or using berries in a vinaigrette can take the acid edge off the vinegar. Symphony and rice wine vinegar make a very good dressing.

SPINACH—Thankfully, spinach is not the centerpiece of many dishes. It can bring out bitter or metallic tastes in wine. Adding cream and Parmesan cheese or a little lemon juice can help soften its flavor.

LEMON JUICE—As with vinegar, it is the acid in citrus juice on its own that poses a problem. However, when combined with other ingredients, the acid is toned down, and lemon juice becomes just another flavor-building component.

FIVE TIPS—OK, SIX TIPS

1. Salty, smoked, spicy, and highly seasoned foods pair best with fruity, lower-alcohol wines like Symphony, rosé and Pinot Noir. Avoid oaky, tannic wines.

2. Richer fatty foods pair best with heavier, full-bodied wines such as Chardonnay, Cabernet Sauvignon, or Merlot.

3. When pairing sweeter foods, try to keep the sweetness of the food less than the apparent sweetness of the wine.

4. Pair highly acidic foods (tomatoes, goat cheese, citrus) with higher acidic wines such as Sauvignon Blanc or Pinot Gris.

5. Try to use the same varietal in your cooking that you want to pair with the course. When buying cooking wine, buy a decent quality. You don't need to break the bank, but if you wouldn't drink the wine there is no reason to believe you will like it any better in the dish.

6. Taste and trust your palate.

OPPOSITE (clockwise): Chef Dan picking fresh herbs in the winery gardens; fresh picked miner's lettuce; watercress grows wild in streams of clear running water; wild turkeys have returned to the Sierra Foothills—they like grapes, too.

Bridge Ingredients

Small adjustments in ingredients can help connect food and wine in flavor, body, intensity or basic taste (bitter, sweet, salty, sour). Here are some bridge ingredients for a selection of common wine varietals.

Symphony—ginger, apricots, vanilla, pears, cloves, cinnamon, orange. *Spicy*—chili powder, chipotle pepper, curry powder, Asian curry paste

Shiraz—caramelized onion, sun-dried tomato, mushrooms, grilled fennel, plums, currants, roasted garlic

Sauvignon Blanc—citrus, bell pepper, crème fraîche, oyster mushrooms, goat cheese

Chardonnay—apples, fennel, tropical fruit, corn, citrus zest, coconut milk, tarragon, Dijon mustard, saffron

Merlot—currants, beets, blackberries, mushrooms, smoked tomatoes

Zinfandel—roasted tomatoes, sun-dried tomatoes, oregano, balsamic vinegar, green peppercorns

Cabernet Franc—raspberries, grilled tomatoes, mint, mushrooms, dried cherries, bay leaf, walnut oil, juniper, tarragon

Cabernet Sauvignon—currants, black pepper, porcini mushrooms, balsamic vinegar, black olives, pecans, blackberries

Sparkling—smoked seafood, caviar, green olives, orange zest

Pairing Wine with Cooking Methods

GRILLING—Grilling involves high heat in direct contact with the food. The outside of the meat is seared, leaving the inside moist and juicy. The caramelization and smoky flavors are intense, so grilled foods prefer bigger, bolder wines with a heavier tannin structure.

ROASTING—Roasting uses a dry heat that caramelizes the outside of your meat and intensifies the flavors on the outside edge as the moisture is cooked out, much like sun-dried fruit or vegetables. The juicy inside meat coats the palate and can soften the tannins of full-bodied red and white wines.

SAUTÉING—Sautéing fish, meat, or vegetables with oil or butter adds richness to your food from the direct contact with the fat. Oaky, buttery Chardonnays enjoy the mouthfeel of that richness.

BRAISING—Braising starts with browning and then enough liquid is added, typically wine and/or stock, to cover the ingredients. This melds the flavors together and lets you use a lot of wine in your preparation, resulting in a happy marriage of food and wine.

OPPOSITE (top): This cluster of Cabernet Franc grapes is ready to become wine. (Bottom): Wine is first fermented in stainless steel tanks then transferred into the wooden barrels for aging.

Recipes *by* Wine Type

CHAMPAGNE AND SPARKLING WINE

CRISP WHITE WINE
(Pinot Grigio, Sauvignon Blanc, Non-Barrel-Fermented Chardonnay, White Rhônes)

BARREL-FERMENTED WHITE WINE
(Fume Blanc, Chardonnay)

LIGHT AND FRUITY WHITE WINE
(Viognier, Chenin Blanc, Chablis)

SEMISWEET WHITE WINE
(Symphony, Riesling, Gewürztraminer)

LIGHT-BODIED RED WINE
(Merlot, Chianti)

MEDIUM-BODIED RED WINE
(Merlot, Cabernet Franc, Pinot Noir, Burgundy, Tempernillo, Sangiovese, Rioja, Zinfandel)

FULL-BODIED RED WINE

(Cabernet Sauvignon, Petit Syrah, Meritage, Bordeaux)

FRUITY RED WINE

(Shiraz, Syrah, Zinfandel, Cabernet Franc, Barbera)

APPETIZERS

BARBECUED OYSTERS

I like to use Pacific oysters for this dish. Their large size and strong, oceany flavor make them perfect for grilling. Look for oysters with closed shells and a fresh, oceany aroma. If the aroma is very strong or they smell fishy, keep walking.

SERVES 8

3/4 CUP BUTTER

1 TABLESPOON CHOPPED SHALLOT

1 TABLESPOON CHOPPED GARLIC

5 TABLESPOONS CHARDONNAY

2 TABLESPOONS FRESHLY SQUEEZED LEMON
    JUICE

2 TABLESPOONS WHOLE-GRAIN MUSTARD

2 TEASPOONS WORCESTERSHIRE SAUCE

1 TEASPOON TABASCO SAUCE

1 1/2 TEASPOONS FRESH ROSEMARY LEAVES

3/4 TEASPOON COARSELY GROUND BLACK PEPPER

SALT

24 OYSTERS, IN SHELLS

1 LEMON, CUT IN 8 WEDGES

MANZANITA OR ROSEMARY SPRIGS FOR
    GARNISH

COMBINE THE BUTTER, shallot, garlic, wine, lemon juice, mustard, Worcestershire sauce, Tabasco sauce, rosemary, and pepper in a medium saucepan. Bring to a boil over high heat, reduce to medium-low heat, and simmer until the butter is completely melted. Season to taste with salt and keep warm until ready to use.

PREHEAT THE GRILL. Wash the oysters under cold running water. Place the oysters on the grill over high heat and cook for 5 minutes, or until the shells start to open. Remove each oyster from the grill when the shell pops open and discard the top shell. (Be sure to use an oven mitt or thick towel to hold the hot oysters.) Return the oysters to the grill and spoon 1 tablespoon of the barbecue sauce onto each oyster. Cook for 1 minute and remove from the grill.

PLACE 3 OYSTER SHELLS on each plate and arrange the lemon wedges and manzanita sprigs around the plate. Drizzle the remaining sauce over the oysters and around the plates.

WINE SUGGESTION: Crisp white wine

GRILLED TOMATO CROSTINI

Grilling the tomatoes gives this crostini its delicious, smoky flavor. Make sure to choose tomatoes that are ripe but still firm so they will retain some of their texture after being grilled. I like to coarsely chop the ingredients for this crostini so you get bursts of different flavors in each bite.

SERVES 8

- 2 RIPE TOMATOES, HALVED AND SEEDED
- 5 TABLESPOONS EXTRA VIRGIN OLIVE OIL
- 1 BAGUETTE FRENCH BREAD
- SALT AND PEPPER
- 1 TEASPOON CHOPPED GARLIC
- 1 TABLESPOON COARSELY CHOPPED FRESH BASIL
- PINCH OF RED PEPPER FLAKES
- 1 TEASPOON CHOPPED SHALLOT
- 1 TABLESPOON BALSAMIC VINEGAR

PREHEAT THE GRILL. Brush the tomatoes with 1 tablespoon of the oil and cook on the hottest area of the grill for 2 to 3 minutes on each side. Cool the tomatoes to room temperature, remove the skins, and coarsely dice.

CUT THE BREAD into 1/4-inch thick slices and brush with 2 tablespoons of the olive oil. Sprinkle the slices with salt and pepper and grill for 2 minutes on each side, or until light golden brown.

COMBINE THE GARLIC, basil, red pepper flakes, shallot, and balsamic vinegar in a small bowl. Slowly whisk in the remaining 2 tablespoons of olive oil and season to taste with salt and pepper. Stir in the diced tomatoes.

SPOON SOME OF THE TOMATO mixture onto each bread slice and serve immediately.

🍇 WINE SUGGESTION: Medium-bodied red wine

TUSCAN-STYLE CANNELLI BEANS WITH SAGE

I developed this dish while preparing for a dinner at the James Beard House in New York. I wanted to use foods that were available in California during the gold rush period and, of course, beans immediately came to mind. Although I doubt any gold miner ever tried it, this is also great with some chopped kalamata olives added just before serving.

SERVES 4

1 POUND CANNELLI BEANS (OR OTHER WHITE BEANS)

SALT

1 TABLESPOON CHOPPED GARLIC

1/2 TEASPOON BLACK PEPPER

1/4 CUP JULIENNED SAGE

7 TABLESPOONS EXTRA VIRGIN OLIVE OIL

1 BAGUETTE FRENCH BREAD

PLACE THE BEANS in a bowl with enough water to cover 1 inch over the beans and soak overnight.

PLACE THE BEANS and water in a saucepan, season with salt, and bring to a boil. Reduce the heat and simmer, stirring occasionally, for 45 minutes to 1 hour, or until the beans are very tender. (Additional water may be added during cooking if the beans become too dry.) Drain the beans, stir in the garlic, and let cool for 5 minutes. Stir in the pepper, sage, and 5 tablespoons of the olive oil. Place one-third of the beans in a small bowl and mash them with a fork. Stir the mashed beans into the whole beans and season to taste with salt.

PREHEAT THE OVEN to 375°. Cut the baguette into 1/4-inch thick slices. Place the slices on a baking sheet, brush with the remaining 2 tablespoons of olive oil, and season with salt and pepper. Toast in the oven for 5 to 7 minutes, or until golden brown.

PLACE THE BEANS in a bowl in the center of a serving platter and arrange the toasted bread slices around the beans.

🍇 WINE SUGGESTION: Barrel-fermented white wine

WATERMELON MARTINIS

I like to serve these martinis to guests as they arrive. They are a wonderful, refreshing starter for a summer party. Served family-style, it is also a great variation on a traditional fruit salad. As an alternative to Ironstone Obsession Symphony, try it with Asti Spumanti instead.

SERVES 6

2 TABLESPOONS FINELY DICED GINGER

1/4 CUP WATER

1/4 CUP SUGAR

4 CUPS DICED WATERMELON, CHILLED

1 TABLESPOON FRESHLY SQUEEZED LIME JUICE

2 TABLESPOONS FINELY CHOPPED MINT

1/2 CUP IRONSTONE OBSESSION SYMPHONY, CHILLED

6 MINT SPRIGS

BLANCH THE GINGER in boiling water and drain. Place the ginger, water, and sugar in a small saucepan and bring to a boil. Cook for 5 minutes then strain through a fine-mesh sieve. Place the candied ginger on waxed paper and let dry for at least 30 minutes.

TOSS TOGETHER THE WATERMELON, candied ginger, lime juice, and mint. Spoon into martini glasses. Pour the wine over the watermelon and garnish with the mint sprigs.

OBSESSION SYMPHONY BY IRONSTONE VINEYARDS
Obsession is the name of the wine, Symphony is the varietal. The symphony grape was first developed at the University of California, Davis in 1948 when Dr. Olmo crossed Muscat of Alexandria with Grenache Gris. The result was a hearty grape with large clusters of large berries that can produce a wine with markedly floral aromas and full fruit flavors. Think honeysuckle and lavender, pineapple and apricot. The wine will tantalize your tongue with illusions of sweetness as it dances across your palate. The sweet acidic balance of this wine makes it a wonderful accompaniment to spicy Asian, Thai and Cajun foods. The clean crisp finish makes it a refreshing drink on those hot afternoons.

GRILLED MUSHROOMS WITH CHÈVRE AND GRILLED TOMATO VINAIGRETTE

Here I used the small portabello mushrooms, but button mushrooms also work well with the chèvre filling. This can easily be made into a salad or first course by doubling the marinade: use 6 large portobellos and serve them on a bed of mixed greens that has been tossed with the extra marinade.

SERVES 6

2 TEASPOONS CHOPPED GARLIC

2 TABLESPOONS CHOPPED FRESH BASIL

PINCH OF RED PEPPER FLAKES

2 TEASPOONS FINELY CHOPPED SHALLOT

2 TABLESPOONS BALSAMIC VINEGAR

1/4 CUP PLUS 2 TABLESPOONS EXTRA VIRGIN OLIVE OIL

SALT AND PEPPER

18 PORTOBELLINI MUSHROOMS, STEMMED

4 RIPE TOMATOES, HALVED

6 OUNCES CHÈVRE

COMBINE THE GARLIC, basil, red pepper, shallot, balsamic vinegar, and 1/4 cup of the olive oil in a large bowl and season to taste with salt and pepper. Toss the mushrooms in the marinade until completely coated and remove with a slotted spoon. Reserve the mushrooms and marinade separately.

PREHEAT THE GRILL. Toss the tomatoes with the remaining 2 tablespoons of olive oil and season with salt and pepper. Grill the tomatoes over high heat for 1 minute on each side. Remove the tomatoes from the grill and refrigerate until chilled.

GRILL THE MUSHROOMS for 2 minutes on each side.

REMOVE THE SKINS from the tomatoes, dice, and toss into the reserved marinade.

SPOON SOME OF THE CHÈVRE into each mushroom cap and top with the diced tomatoes.

🍇 WINE SUGGESTION: Medium-bodied or fruity red wine

Shrimp and Scallop Ceviche

A true ceviche would use raw scallops and shrimp and allow the acid in the lime juice to cook them. But, because people often get a little squeamish about raw seafood, I have blanched them before tossing them with the other ingredients. The light, fresh flavors of this ceviche make it a great alternative to salsa.

Serves 8

8 OUNCES SEA SCALLOPS, SLICED $1/4$ INCH THICK

8 OUNCES MEDIUM SHRIMP, PEELED, DEVEINED, AND HALVED LENGTHWISE

$2/3$ CUP FRESHLY SQUEEZED LIME JUICE

$1/4$ CUP JULIENNED RED BELL PEPPER

$1/4$ CUP JULIENNED RED ONION

2 AVOCADOS, PEELED AND DICED

14 CHERRY TOMATOES, HALVED

3 JALAPEÑO PEPPERS, SEEDED AND FINELY DICED

$1/4$ CUP CHOPPED CILANTRO

$1/4$ CUP EXTRA VIRGIN OLIVE OIL

$1 1/2$ TEASPOONS SALT

TORTILLAS CHIPS

BRING A POT OF SALTED WATER to a boil and add the scallops and shrimp. Cook for 2 minutes, drain, and cool to room temperature.

GENTLY TOSS THE SCALLOPS and shrimp with the lime juice, red pepper, onion, avocados, tomatoes, jalapeños, cilantro, olive oil, and salt in a nonreactive bowl, being careful not to smash the avocado. Refrigerate for at least 2 hours, or overnight.

DRAIN HALF OF THE JUICE and discard. Serve the ceviche in a bowl with the tortilla chips on the side.

WINE SUGGESTION: Light and fruity or semisweet white wine

SIX-ONION TARTS WITH WILD MUSHROOMS AND GRUYÈRE

The variety of onions in this tart add a depth of flavor that cannot be achieved using only one type of onion. I usually prepare this as four large tarts, but it can easily be adapted for a buffet table by cutting each of the puff pastry squares in quarters, resulting in sixteen bite-sized tarts.

SERVES 4

1 PUFF PASTRY SHEET, QUARTERED

1 EGG, BEATEN

1 CUP THINLY SLICED WILD MUSHROOMS

1/4 CUP BUTTER

SALT AND PEPPER

1/2 YELLOW ONION, JULIENNED

1/2 RED ONION, JULIENNED

1/2 CUP CHOPPED LEEK

1/4 CUP CHOPPED SHALLOTS

1/2 TEASPOON CHOPPED GARLIC

1 TEASPOON FRESH THYME LEAVES

1 TABLESPOON FLOUR

1 TABLESPOON IRONSTONE OBSESSION SYMPHONY

1/4 CUP WHIPPING CREAM

2 GREEN ONIONS, CHOPPED

1 TABLESPOON CHOPPED CHIVES

4 SLICES GRUYÈRE CHEESE

1 TABLESPOON GRATED ROMANO CHEESE

FOLD UP 1/2-INCH STRIPS on each side of the puff pastry squares, pinching the corners together to hold up the sides and form an edge. Place the puff pastry on a parchment-lined baking pan, brush with the egg, and refrigerate until ready to use.

COOK THE MUSHROOMS and 1 tablespoon of the butter in a large sauté pan over medium heat for 10 minutes, or until all of the moisture has evaporated. Season to taste with salt and pepper, remove the mushrooms from the pan, and set aside.

ADD THE YELLOW ONION, red onion, leek, shallots, and the remaining 3 tablespoons of butter to the pan and cook for 10 minutes, or until the onions are soft. Add the garlic and thyme and cook for 5 minutes, or until the onions just begin to brown. Add the flour and cook for 1 minute. Add the wine and cook for 1 minute. Add the cream and cook for 5 minutes, or until thick. Remove from the heat, stir in the green onions and chives, and season to taste with salt and pepper.

PREHEAT THE OVEN TO 375°. Place 1 slice of Gruyère cheese in the center of each puff pastry square. Spoon a layer of mushrooms on the cheese and top with the onion mixture. Sprinkle the Romano cheese over the onions and bake for 10 to 15 minutes, or until the pastry is golden brown.

WINE SUGGESTION: Barrel-fermented or semisweet white wine

GRILLED POLENTA WITH HOMEMADE ITALIAN SAUSAGE

Making your own Italian sausage may seem extreme, but it takes about five minutes and it can't be matched with store-bought. The flavor of the fresh sausage combined with the polenta and peppers is an unbeatable combination. At the winery I usually serve this as an appetizer, but for me it could be the whole meal (and usually is).

SERVES 8

2 TABLESPOONS MINCED ONION

1 SMALL GARLIC CLOVE, MINCED

1 TABLESPOON BUTTER

1 CUP CHICKEN STOCK

1/4 CUP MILK

1/2 CUP POLENTA

3/4 CUP GRATED ROMANO CHEESE

SALT AND PEPPER

1/2 RED BELL PEPPER, JULIENNED

1/2 YELLOW BELL PEPPER, JULIENNED

1 SMALL ONION, CHOPPED

2 TABLESPOONS OLIVE OIL

1 TEASPOON CHOPPED GARLIC

1 LARGE TOMATO, PEELED, SEEDED, AND DICED

2 TEASPOONS CHOPPED FRESH OREGANO

1 TABLESPOON CHOPPED FRESH BASIL

1 1/2 POUNDS ITALIAN SAUSAGE (RECIPE FOLLOWS)

8 SMALL BASIL SPRIGS

SAUTÉ THE MINCED ONION and minced garlic in the butter in a small saucepan for 2 minutes. Add the chicken stock and milk and bring to a boil. Add the polenta and simmer, stirring frequently, for 15 minutes, or until thick. Remove from the heat, stir in 1/4 cup of the Romano cheese, and season to taste with salt and pepper. Evenly spread the polenta in an 8-inch square baking pan and cool to room temperature. Cover with plastic wrap and refrigerate until thoroughly chilled.

SAUTÉ THE RED PEPPER, yellow pepper, and onion in the olive oil for 8 to 10 minutes, or until soft. Add the chopped garlic and tomato and cook for 2 minutes. Remove from the heat and stir in the oregano and basil. Season to taste with salt and pepper and keep warm.

FORM THE ITALIAN SAUSAGE into 24 2-inch-diameter patties. Cook the sausage patties over medium heat for 3 to 4 minutes on each side, or until thoroughly cooked. Drain on paper towels and keep warm.

PREHEAT THE GRILL. Cut the chilled polenta into quarters and grill for 2 minutes. Carefully turn over the polenta and cook for 1 minute. Remove from the grill and cut each quarter into 6 pieces.

ALTERNATE 3 OF THE POLENTA pieces and 3 sausage patties in the center of each plate and top with some of the sautéed pepper mixture. Sprinkle with the remaining 1/2 cup of Romano cheese and garnish with a basil sprig.

🍇 WINE SUGGESTION: Medium-bodied red wine

Italian Sausage

MAKES 2¹/₂ POUNDS

2¹/₂ POUNDS GROUND PORK BUTT OR SHOULDER

2 TABLESPOONS MINCED RED BELL PEPPER

1 TABLESPOON MINCED GARLIC

1 TABLESPOON WHOLE FENNEL SEEDS

¹/₂ TEASPOON RED PEPPER FLAKES

2 TEASPOONS COARSELY GROUND BLACK PEPPER

1 TABLESPOON PLUS ¹/₂ TEASPOON KOSHER SALT

¹/₄ CUP COLD WATER

PLACE ALL OF THE INGREDIENTS in a large bowl and knead until thoroughly combined. (Cook a small piece of sausage right away to make sure the seasoning is correct.) Keep refrigerated until ready to use. Extra sausage may be frozen for up to 2 months.

FRIED CALAMARI WITH CHIPOTLE DIPPING SAUCE

This sauce is not for the faint of heart! The chipotle peppers not only impart a wonderful smokey flavor, they also add some serious heat. If you aren't up for a five-alarm experience, purée a roasted red bell pepper or two into the sauce to tone down the heat.

SERVES 4

7 OUNCES CHIPOTLE PEPPERS IN ADOBO SAUCE

1/2 CUP HONEY

2 TABLESPOONS PICKLED GINGER JUICE

PEANUT OIL FOR FRYING

2 POUNDS CALAMARI, CLEANED AND CUT IN RINGS

FLOUR FOR DREDGING

SALT AND PEPPER

4 OUNCES PICKLED GINGER

PURÉE THE CHIPOTLE PEPPERS and their sauce with the honey and pickled ginger juice until smooth. Refrigerate until ready to serve.

POUR 3 INCHES OF THE PEANUT OIL in a large saucepan and heat to 350°. Dredge the calamari in the flour, shaking off any excess. Carefully drop the calamari into the hot oil and fry for 30 seconds, or until lightly browned. Remove with a slotted spoon and drain on paper towels. Season to taste with salt and pepper.

PLACE THE SAUCE in a small bowl in the center of a serving platter. Arrange the calamari and pickled ginger around the sauce and serve immediately.

WINE SUGGESTION: Semisweet white wine

HERBED CHEESE ROLLS

These are a great finger food for parties. They are simple to put together and can be prepared well in advance and just baked at the last moment. Prosciutto, Gruyère, and herbes de Provence are always a great combination, but almost any mixture of thinly sliced meats and cheeses works well.

SERVES 6

1 PUFF PASTRY SHEET

2 TABLESPOONS DIJON MUSTARD

2 TEASPOONS HERBES DE PROVENCE

8 THIN SLICES PROSCIUTTO

6 SLICES GRUYÈRE CHEESE

LAY THE SHEET of puff pastry on a piece of plastic wrap. Spread the Dijon mustard on the puff pastry, leaving a $1/2$-inch strip at the top to seal the roll. Sprinkle the herbes de Provence over the mustard. Place the prosciutto over the herbs and top with the cheese slices. Roll up the puff pastry as tight as possible, pressing firmly to seal the top edge. Wrap the roll in the plastic wrap and refrigerate for at least 30 minutes. (The rolls may be kept in the refrigerator for up to 2 days or frozen for up to 2 months.)

PREHEAT THE OVEN to 400°. With the plastic wrap on, cut the roll into scant $1/2$-inch-thick slices. Remove the plastic wrap from each slice and place on a parchment-lined baking sheet. Bake for 8 to 10 minutes, or until the edges are golden brown. Place on a serving tray and serve warm.

🍇 WINE SUGGESTION: Barrel-fermented white wine or medium-bodied red wine

Pan-Seared Prawns with Orange-Cilantro Sauce

Although this sauce contains jalapeño, it is not particularly spicy. Because the jalapeño is cooked and then paired with the sweet orange juice and cream, the sauce retains the flavor of the pepper without the heat. If you prefer a little more zip, you can stir in a little fresh jalapeño with the cilantro.

SERVES 4

ZEST OF 2 ORANGES

1 CUP WATER

1/2 CUP SUGAR

2 TABLESPOONS CHILI POWDER

1 TABLESPOON GARLIC POWDER

1 TABLESPOON CUMIN

1 TEASPOON SALT

1 TEASPOON BLACK PEPPER

1 TEASPOON WHITE PEPPER

1 TEASPOON DRIED MEXICAN OREGANO

1/2 TEASPOON CINNAMON

12 JUMBO PRAWNS, PEELED AND DEVEINED

2 TABLESPOONS CANOLA OIL

1 JALAPEÑO, SEEDED AND MINCED

1/4 TEASPOON MINCED SHALLOT

1/4 TEASPOON MINCED GARLIC

1 CUP FRESHLY SQUEEZED ORANGE JUICE

1 CUP WHIPPING CREAM

1/4 CUP BUTTER, AT ROOM TEMPERATURE

2 TABLESPOONS CHOPPED CILANTRO

4 CILANTRO SPRIGS

BLANCH THE ORANGE ZEST in boiling water and drain through a fine-mesh sieve. Bring the 1 cup of water and the sugar to a boil. Add the orange zest and simmer for 5 minutes. Drain through a fine-mesh sieve and spread the zest on waxed paper to cool.

COMBINE THE CHILI POWDER, garlic powder, cumin, salt, black pepper, white pepper, oregano, and cinnamon in a small bowl. Dredge the prawns in the spice mixture, shaking off any excess.

HEAT THE OIL in a skillet over medium-high heat. Add the prawns and cook for 1 minute on each side, or until firm. Remove from the skillet and keep warm.

DISCARD HALF OF THE OIL from the pan, add the jalapeño and shallot, and cook for 1 minute, stirring often to prevent browning. Add the garlic and cook for 30 seconds. Add the orange juice and cook for 5 to 6 minutes, or until reduced to about 1/2 cup. Add the cream and cook for 6 to 7 minutes, or until reduced to about 3/4 cup. Remove the pan from the heat and whisk in the butter, one-third at a time. Stir in the cilantro and season to taste with salt and pepper.

STAND 3 PRAWNS in the center of each bowl and spoon some of the sauce over the prawns. Sprinkle with the orange zest and garnish with the cilantro sprigs.

🍇 WINE SUGGESTION: Crisp white wine

DAN'S MARINATED MUSSELS

This is a perfect early course for a dinner party. It is light and flavorful and can be completely prepared up to a day in advance. It is also great served family-style with toasted garlic bread to soak up any remaining marinade.

SERVES 4

MUSSELS

1 TABLESPOON CHOPPED GARLIC

1 TABLESPOON CHOPPED SHALLOT

1 TABLESPOON EXTRA VIRGIN OLIVE OIL

2 POUNDS MUSSELS, CLEANED AND DEBEARDED

2 TABLESPOONS FRESHLY SQUEEZED LEMON JUICE

2 TABLESPOONS CHARDONNAY

MARINADE

2 TABLESPOONS MUSSEL COOKING LIQUID

1 1/2 TEASPOONS CHOPPED GARLIC

1 TABLESPOON CHOPPED SHALLOT

3 TABLESPOONS EXTRA VIRGIN OLIVE OIL

3 TABLESPOONS FRESHLY SQUEEZED LEMON JUICE

1/2 CUP CHARDONNAY

2 TEASPOONS CHOPPED PARSLEY

1 TEASPOON FRESHLY GROUND BLACK PEPPER

2 TABLESPOONS SHERRY VINEGAR

1/2 TEASPOON HONEY

1/8 TEASPOON SEA SALT

PINCH OF CRUSHED RED PEPPER

4 LARGE LEAF LETTUCE LEAVES

TO PREPARE THE MUSSELS: Place the garlic, shallot, and olive oil in a large sauté pan over medium heat and cook for 3 minutes, or until the shallots are translucent. Add the mussels, lemon juice, and wine, cover, and cook for 1 minute, or until the mussels open. Remove the from the heat and cool in the pan.

TO PREPARE THE MARINADE: Combine the marinade ingredients in a large bowl. Remove the mussels from their shells, reserving one-fourth of the best shells. Add the mussels to the marinade and refrigerate for 1 hour, or until thoroughly chilled.

PLACE A PIECE OF LEAF LETTUCE in the center of each plate. Spoon 2 mussels into each shell and fill the shells with the marinade. Arrange the mussel shells on top of the lettuce and serve immediately.

WINE SUGGESTION: Crisp white wine

MISSION FIGS with PANCETTA and BALSAMIC VINEGAR

This is a classic example of the saying, the whole exceeds the sum of its parts. Each ingredient is good by itself, but together they become an incredible combination of flavors and textures that your guests are sure to love. After tasting this, no one will believe how simple it is to prepare, so I say, don't tell 'em.

SERVES 4

- 1/4 CUP FINELY DICED PANCETTA
- 4 LEAF LETTUCE LEAVES
- 8 RIPE MISSION FIGS, QUARTERED
- 1 TABLESPOON FINELY CHOPPED SAGE

- 1/2 CUP TOASTED WALNUT HALVES
- 1/4 CUP WALNUT OIL
- 4 TEASPOONS BALSAMIC VINEGAR
- SEA SALT AND PEPPER

SAUTÉ THE PANCETTA over medium heat for 5 minutes, or until crispy.

PLACE THE LEAF LETTUCE in the center of a serving platter. Arrange the figs on the lettuce in a star pattern. Sprinkle the sage, walnuts, and pancetta over the figs. Drizzle with the walnut oil and balsamic vinegar. Sprinkle with sea salt and pepper.

🍇 WINE SUGGESTION: Medium-bodied red wine

CHICKEN ROULADE with WILTED ARUGULA and FERMENTED BLACK BEAN DEMI-GLACE

This dish is guaranteed to impress your guests, but better yet, it is very easy to prepare and all of the prep work can be done well ahead of time. The fermented black beans used in the sauce are small black soy beans that have been preserved in salt. They may also be called Chinese black beans or salty black beans and can be found in any Asian market and in many grocery stores.

SERVES 8

- ½ CUP JULIENNED PORTOBELLO MUSHROOMS
- ½ CUP DICED SHIITAKE MUSHROOMS
- ½ CUP DICED OYSTER MUSHROOMS
- ¼ CUP BUTTER
- ¼ CUP EXTRA VIRGIN OLIVE OIL
- 1 TEASPOON FRESH THYME
- 2 TABLESPOONS MINCED SHALLOT
- 1 TEASPOON MINCED GARLIC

- 1 CUP DICED DARK CHICKEN MEAT
- ½ CUP WHIPPING CREAM
- SALT AND PEPPER
- 4 CHICKEN BREASTS
- 1½ POUNDS ARUGULA, WASHED AND TRIMMED
- ⅓ CUP JULIENNED SUN-DRIED TOMATOES
- FERMENTED BLACK BEAN DEMI-GLACE (RECIPE FOLLOWS)

SAUTÉ THE PORTOBELLO, shiitake, and oyster mushrooms in 2 tablespoons of the butter and 2 tablespoons of the olive oil for 5 minutes, or until tender. Add the thyme, shallot, and garlic and cook for 2 minutes. Remove from the heat and cool.

PURÉE THE DARK CHICKEN meat in a food processor. Add 1 tablespoon of the butter and blend until thoroughly combined. Slowly add the cream and blend until completely incorporated. Fold in the mushroom mixture and season with salt and pepper.

PREHEAT THE OVEN to 350°. Slice the chicken breasts lengthwise, almost all the way through, and open them like a book. Cover with plastic wrap and pound with a meat mallet until ¼ to ½ inch thick. Spread a single layer of arugula leaves on each breast, leaving the back 2 inches uncovered. Spread one-quarter of the chicken mixture over each breast

and top with the sun-dried tomatoes. Roll the chicken breasts to form 4 logs. Place the rolls on a baking sheet seam side down. Melt the remaining 1 tablespoon of butter and brush over the chicken. Season with salt and pepper and bake for 20 to 25 minutes, or until the chicken is done. Let rest for 10 minutes and cut each roulade into 6 slices.

HEAT THE REMAINING 2 tablespoons of the olive oil in a large sauté pan over medium-high heat. Add the remaining arugula and cook for 1 minute, or until just wilted. Season with salt and pepper.

PLACE SOME OF THE ARUGULA in the center of each plate. Arrange the roulade slices on the arugula and drizzle the demi-glace and around the plate.

🍇 WINE SUGGESTION: Full-bodied red wine

Fermented Black Bean Demi-Glace

MAKES 1 CUP

¹/₂ TEASPOON GRATED GINGER

2 TABLESPOONS CRUSHED FERMENTED BLACK BEANS

1¹/₂ TEASPOONS BUTTER

¹/₂ CUP CABERNET SAUVIGNON

1¹/₄ CUPS DEMI-GLACE

2 TABLESPOONS SOY SAUCE

SALT AND PEPPER

SAUTÉ THE GINGER and black beans in the butter in a small saucepan over medium heat for 2 minutes. Add the wine and cook for 5 minutes, or until reduced to about ¹/₄ cup. Add the demi-glace and soy sauce, lower the heat, and simmer for 20 minutes, or until reduced to about 1 cup. Season to taste with salt and pepper.

HOT SMOKED SALMON IN SAVORY PASTRY CUPS

This style of curing adds great flavor to the salmon and it also has the side benefit of forming a pellicle, or outer skin, on the fillet. This makes it easier to smoke the fish without it breaking apart. If the idea of smoking salmon is overwhelming, you can use store-bought smoked salmon for this recipe, but I recommend you give it a try. It is easier than you might think and deliciously rewarding.

SERVES 12

CURE

4 CUPS BROWN SUGAR

2 CUPS KOSHER SALT

1 CUP PAPRIKA

1/2 CUP GROUND CUMIN

1/4 CUP MEXICAN OREGANO

1/2 CUP CHILI POWDER

1 TABLESPOON GROUND CELERY SEED

3-TO 4-POUND SALMON FILLET,
   SKIN REMOVED

PASTRY

1/2 CUP BUTTER

1 CUP WATER

1 CUP FLOUR

1/2 TEASPOON SALT

4 EGGS

1 TABLESPOON HERBES DE PROVENCE

1 TEASPOON MINCED GARLIC

16 OUNCES CREAM CHEESE

1/4 CUP DICED RED ONION

6 CUPS WOOD CHIPS (SUCH AS APPLE, CHERRY, OR HICKORY)

48 CAPERBERRIES

COMBINE THE BROWN SUGAR, kosher salt, paprika, cumin, oregano, chili powder, and celery seed in a large bowl. Place one half of the mixture in a baking pan and top with the salmon. Cover the salmon with the remaining spice mixture and pat down to insure it is completely covered. Cover with plastic wrap and refrigerate for at least 8 hours, or overnight.

PREHEAT THE OVEN to 425°. Bring the butter and water to a boil in a large saucepan. Add the flour and salt all at once and cook over medium heat, stirring constantly, for 5 minutes, or until the mixture leaves the sides of the pan and forms a stiff ball. Remove the pan from the heat and add the eggs, one at a time, stirring well after each addition. Add the herbes de Provence and garlic and stir well. Drop the dough into 24 golf ball–sized mounds placed about 3 inches apart on ungreased baking sheets. Bake for 30 to 35 minutes, or until golden brown. Cool to room temperature and slice each pastry puff in half.

COMBINE THE CREAM CHEESE and red onion in a small bowl and set aside.

HEAT THE GRILL (or smoker) with the coals banked around the edges and the grates removed. Rinse the salmon under running water until most of the cure is removed, and pat dry. (The salmon will retain the red color from the paprika.) Place half of the wood chips on the hot coals and place the grates on the grill. Place the salmon in the center of the grates and cover immediately. Smoke the salmon for 10 to 15 minutes, or until the smokes starts to diminish. Add the remaining wood chips, turn over the salmon, and continue smoking for 10 to 15 minutes, or until the salmon is just barely cooked. Remove from the grill and keep warm until ready to serve. (The salmon can also be served at room temperature.)

SPREAD A THIN LAYER of the cream cheese on each of the cream puff halves. Top with some of the smoked salmon and a small dollop of the cream cheese mixture. Place a caperberry on top of the cream cheese and arrange on a serving tray.

🍇 WINE SUGGESTION: Barrel-fermented or semisweet white wine

VERMOUTH-BRINED GRILLED QUAIL WITH QUAIL SPRING ROLL AND FIVE SPICE–VERMOUTH PLUM SAUCE

Although this recipe sounds complicated, it is a great dish to make for guests. All of the components can be prepared ahead of time and then be finished just prior to serving. This dish can be served as an appetizer for eight or as an entrée for four.

SERVES 8

QUAIL

8 WHOLE QUAIL, BONED

1/4 CUP SUGAR

1/4 CUP SALT

2 TABLESPOONS CHINESE FIVE SPICE

2 CUPS SWEET VERMOUTH

2 CUPS WATER

SPRING ROLLS

QUAIL TRIMMINGS FROM LEG AND THIGH, FINELY CHOPPED

1 1/4 CUPS SHREDDED CABBAGE

1/3 CUP SHREDDED CARROT

1/4 CUP JULIENNED RED ONION

1/4 CUP CHOPPED GREEN ONION

2 TABLESPOONS CHOPPED CILANTRO

1 TABLESPOON MINCED GINGER

1/2 TEASPOON CHINESE FIVE SPICE

1 CUP PLUS 1 TABLESPOON FIVE SPICE–VERMOUTH PLUM SAUCE, WARM (RECIPE FOLLOWS)

1/2 TEASPOON SOY SAUCE

SALT AND PEPPER

8 LARGE RICE PAPER SKINS

CANOLA OIL FOR FRYING

8 RED SWISS CHARD LEAVES

1 GREEN ONION, THINLY SLICED ON THE DIAGONAL

1/2 TEASPOON RED PEPPERCORN FLAKES

SLICE THE QUAIL BREASTS apart and remove the legs and thighs. Remove the skin and meat from the legs and thighs and reserve for the spring rolls. Combine the sugar, salt, five spice, vermouth, and water in a bowl and stir until the salt and sugar are dissolved. Add the quail, cover with plastic wrap, and refrigerate for 2 hours.

COOK THE QUAIL TRIMMINGS in a small sauté pan over high heat for 3 to 5 minutes, or until browned. Combine the quail trimmings, cabbage,

carrot, red onion, green onion, cilantro, ginger, five spice, 1 tablespoon of the Five Spice–Vermouth Plum Sauce, and the soy sauce in a bowl and season to taste with salt and pepper. Soak 1 sheet of the rice paper at a time in warm water for 1 minute. Remove the rice paper from the water and pat dry. Spoon some of the filling across one corner of each rice paper sheet, fold in the sides, and roll into a tight cigar shape. (The spring rolls can be wrapped in plastic wrap and refrigerated for up to 4 hours.)

continued

POUR 2 INCHES OF OIL into a saucepan and heat to 350°. Cook the spring rolls in the oil for 2 to 3 minutes, or until golden brown. Remove from the oil and drain on paper towels.

PREHEAT THE GRILL. Remove the quail from the marinade and cook for 2 to 3 minutes on each side, or until done. Let rest for 5 minutes and cut each piece in half.

PLACE A SWISS CHARD LEAF on each plate and arrange 2 quail pieces on one side of the plate. Spoon some of the remaining sauce into small dipping bowls and place next to the quail. Cut each of the spring rolls in half on the diagonal. Lay one half next to the sauce and stand the other half upright next to the quail. Sprinkle the green onion and red peppercorns over the quail and spring rolls and drizzle some of the sauce around the plates.

NOTE: *Five spice is a mixture of ground spices usually consisting of equal parts of fennel seed, cinnamon, star anise, clove, and Szechuan peppercorns. It is used extensively in Chinese cooking and can be found in most supermarkets.*

WINE SUGGESTION: Semisweet white wine

Five Spice–Vermouth Plum Sauce
MAKES 1 1/4 CUPS

2 CUPS CHOPPED RIPE PLUMS (OR RECONSTITUTED DRIED PLUMS)

1/2 CUP HONEY

1/4 CUP SWEET VERMOUTH

2 TABLESPOONS FRESHLY SQUEEZED ORANGE JUICE

2 TABLESPOONS FRESHLY SQUEEZED LEMON JUICE

2 TEASPOONS MINCED RED ONION

1 TEASPOON ORANGE ZEST

1/2 TEASPOON MINCED GINGER

1/2 TEASPOON CHINESE FIVE SPICE

SALT AND PEPPER

COMBINE ALL OF THE INGREDIENTS in a small saucepan over high heat and bring to a boil. Lower the heat to medium-low and simmer for 20 minutes. Purée the mixture in a blender until smooth and season to taste with additional salt, pepper, and honey, if necessary. Return the purée to the saucepan and simmer for 15 minutes, or until reduced to about 1 1/4 cups.

POLENTA AND GOAT CHEESE TARTS

These delicious little tarts are great for a buffet table or hors d'ouevres tray. They can be prepared several hours ahead and baked just prior to serving. Choose the type of goat cheese you use according to your tastes. Fresh goat cheese will provide a very mild flavor whereas an aged goat cheese will have a sharper, nuttier flavor.

SERVES 8

1 TABLESPOON MINCED ONION

1 SMALL GARLIC CLOVE, MINCED

3 TABLESPOONS BUTTER

$1/2$ CUP CHICKEN STOCK

2 TABLESPOONS MILK

$1/4$ CUP POLENTA

SALT AND PEPPER

3 READY-MADE PIE CRUSTS

8 OUNCES WILD MUSHROOMS, SLICED

1 TABLESPOON MINCED SHALLOT

$1/4$ CUP SOUR CREAM

5 OUNCES GOAT CHEESE, CRUMBLED OR GRATED

1 EGG

1 TABLESPOON CHOPPED PROSCIUTTO

1 TABLESPOON THYME LEAVES

6 SLICES PROSCIUTTO, QUARTERED

SAUTÉ THE ONION and garlic in 1 tablespoon of the butter in a small saucepan for 2 minutes. Add the chicken stock and milk and bring to a boil. Add the polenta and simmer, stirring frequently, for 15 minutes, or until thick. Remove from the heat, season to taste with salt and pepper, and cool to room temperature.

CUT THE PIE CRUSTS into 24 3-inch circles. Press the dough circles into 2-inch tart rings (or mini muffin tins).

PREHEAT THE OVEN to 350°. Sauté the mushrooms in the remaining 2 tablespoons of butter for 10 minutes, or until they begin to brown. Remove the pan from the heat and stir in the shallot. Spoon some of the mushroom mixture in the bottom of each tart shell and bake for 7 minutes.

PUSH THE POLENTA through a food mill or potato ricer and combine with the sour cream. Add the goat cheese to the polenta, stir in the egg and chopped prosciutto, and season with salt and pepper. Spread the polenta mixture over the mushrooms and sprinkle with the thyme leaves. Fold the prosciutto pieces into quarters and insert one piece into each tart. (If desired, the tarts may be refrigerated at this point for several hours before final baking.) Bake for 20 to 25 minutes, or until the polenta rises and turns golden brown.

🍇 WINE SUGGESTION: Barrel-fermented or light and fruity white wine

SOUPS & SALADS

ONION SOUP

I like to use a variety of onions, but even when using only one type, this is a good soup! The combination of beef and chicken stock gives the broth a rich flavor that is perfect with the cheese croutons. In fact, I usually make extra croutons and serve them on the side for dipping.

SERVES 6

- 1/2 CUP PLUS 2 TABLESPOONS BUTTER
- 1 RED ONION, JULIENNED
- 1 YELLOW ONION, JULIENNED
- 1/2 CUP JULIENNED SHALLOTS
- 1/2 TEASPOON THYME
- 6 BAY LEAVES (OR 1 FRESH BAY LEAF)
- 6 GREEN ONIONS, CHOPPED, GREEN AND WHITE PARTS SEPARATED
- 1 TABLESPOON CHOPPED GARLIC
- 1 CUP SHERRY
- 1 QUART BEEF STOCK
- 1 QUART CHICKEN STOCK
- 1 BEEF BOUILLON CUBE
- 1 CHICKEN BOUILLON CUBE
- SALT AND PEPPER
- 1/2 CUP WHIPPING CREAM
- 1/2 CUP GRATED GRUYÈRE CHEESE
- 1/2 CUP GRATED ROMANO OR PARMESAN CHEESE
- 6 1/4-INCH-THICK SLICES FRENCH BREAD

MELT 1/2 CUP OF THE BUTTER in a large saucepan over medium heat. Add the red onion, yellow onion, shallots, thyme, bay leaves, and the white part of the green onions. Cook, stirring frequently, for 15 minutes or until the onions are soft and begin to brown. Add the garlic and cook, stirring frequently, for 10 minutes. Add the sherry, stir well to loosen any onions that might be stuck to the pan, and cook for 10 minutes. Add the beef stock, chicken stock, beef bouillon cube, and chicken bouillon cube and bring to a boil. Reduce the heat to medium-low and simmer for 1 hour. Season to taste with salt and pepper. Remove from the heat and stir in the cream and green onion tops just prior to serving.

PREHEAT THE OVEN to 400°. Combine the Gruyère and Romano cheeses. If necessary, trim the bread slices to fit the size of your bowls. Lightly butter one side of each bread slice with the remaining 2 tablespoons of butter. Place the bread on a baking sheet, buttered side up, and top with the cheese mixture. Bake for 5 minutes, or until the bread is toasted and cheese starts to brown.

LADLE THE SOUP into bowls and top each bowl with a cheese crouton.

WINE SUGGESTION: Barrel-fermented white wine or medium-bodied red wine

White Bean Chicken Chili with Jalapeño Cornbread Muffins

I originally developed this recipe to take to the Reno Chili Cookoff. Being from a winery, I felt that my chili needed to be wine friendly and this version pairs beautifully with Chardonnay. For added flavor, you can place a piece of jalapeño or a cube of Jack cheese on top of each muffin before baking.

Serves 6 to 8

1 POUND CANNELLI OR NAVY BEANS

1 POUND BONELESS, SKINLESS CHICKEN BREASTS

1 1/2 TABLESPOONS EXTRA VIRGIN OLIVE OIL

1/2 CUP DICED ONION

2 TABLESPOONS DICED JALAPEÑO

1 1/2 TABLESPOONS MINCED GARLIC

1/4 CUP ROASTED GREEN CHILES

1 TABLESPOON MEXICAN OREGANO

3/4 TEASPOON GROUND CUMIN

6 CUPS CHICKEN STOCK

SALT

JALAPEÑO CORNBREAD MUFFINS (RECIPE FOLLOWS)

PLACE THE BEANS in a bowl with enough water to cover 1 inch over the beans and soak overnight.

CUT THE CHICKEN into 1-inch pieces and sauté in the olive oil in a large saucepan over medium-high heat for 3 minutes. Add the onion and jalapeño and cook over medium heat for 5 to 7 minutes, or until the onions are soft but not brown. Add the garlic, chiles, oregano, and cumin and cook for 1 minute.

Add the chicken stock and the beans and their soaking liquid. Bring to a boil and reduce to medium heat. Cover and simmer for 90 minutes, or until the beans are tender and the chicken flakes apart. Season to taste with salt and serve with the Jalapeño Cornbread Muffins.

 WINE SUGGESTION: Barrel-fermented white wine

Jalapeño Cornbread Muffins

MAKES 12 TO 18 MUFFINS

1/2 CUP CORNMEAL

1 1/2 CUPS FLOUR

2/3 CUP SUGAR

1 TABLESPOON BAKING POWDER

1/2 TEASPOON SALT

1 SLICE BACON, DICED

1 JALAPEÑO, SEEDED AND CHOPPED

1 TABLESPOON FINELY CHOPPED ONION

1 TABLESPOON FINELY CHOPPED
   GREEN BELL PEPPER

2/3 CUP FRESH CORN KERNELS

1/3 CUP UNSALTED BUTTER

2 EGGS

1 CUP MILK

COMBINE THE CORNMEAL, flour, sugar, baking powder, and salt in a large bowl and set aside.

COOK THE BACON in a small sauté pan over medium-low heat for 5 to 7 minutes, or until cooked, but not brown. Add the jalapeño, onion, green pepper, corn kernels, and butter and cook for 5 minutes, or until the onions are tender. Remove from the heat and cool slightly.

PREHEAT THE OVEN to 375°. Lightly grease a muffin pan. Whisk together the eggs and milk and add the bacon mixture. Pour the egg mixture into the cornmeal mixture and stir until just combined. Fill each muffin cup two-thirds full with the batter. Bake for 18 to 20 minutes, or until golden brown and the muffins spring back when lightly pressed.

CLAM CHOWDER

Growing up in Monterey, I often made clam chowder from the clams we dug up along the coast. In fact, it seems like I've been making clam chowder my whole life, but after I learned to cook professionally I started making really good clam chowder. A bowl of steaming clam chowder and a loaf of crusty sourdough bread—it doesn't get much better than that.

SERVES 4

- 1/2 CUP DICED BACON
- 2 TABLESPOONS BUTTER
- 2/3 CUP DICED RED ONION
- 2 TABLESPOONS DICED GREEN BELL PEPPER
- 1/4 CUP DICED LEEK
- 1/4 CUP DICED CELERY
- 2 TABLESPOONS CHOPPED GARLIC
- 2 TEASPOONS DRIED THYME
- PINCH OF DRIED OREGANO
- PINCH OF DRIED BASIL
- 2 BAY LEAVES

- 2 TEASPOONS COARSELY GROUND BLACK PEPPER
- 1/2 CUP FLOUR
- 2 1/2 CUPS MILK
- 2 CUPS DICED RED POTATO
- 24 OUNCES CHOPPED CLAMS IN JUICE
- 1 TEASPOON TABASCO SAUCE
- DASH OF WORCESTERSHIRE SAUCE
- 1 TABLESPOON FRESHLY SQUEEZED LEMON JUICE
- 16 FRESH MANILA CLAMS, IN SHELLS
- 2 CUPS WHIPPING CREAM
- SALT AND PEPPER

SAUTÉ THE BACON in the butter for 3 minutes, or until the bacon is softened but not brown. Add the onion, green bell pepper, leek, celery, garlic, thyme, oregano, basil, bay leaves, and coarsely ground pepper and sauté for 5 minutes, or until the vegetables are tender. Gently stir in the flour and cook over low heat for 5 minutes, stirring frequently to prevent browning.

ADD THE MILK, potato, chopped clams, Tabasco sauce, Worcestershire sauce, and lemon juice and stir well. Simmer over medium-low heat, stirring frequently, for 15 to 20 minutes, or until the potatoes are tender.

ADD THE FRESH CLAMS and cook for 3 to 5 minutes, or until the clamshells are open. Remove the pan from the heat and add the cream. Season to taste with salt and pepper and serve immediately.

WINE SUGGESTION: Barrel-fermented white wine

CURRIED PUMPKIN SOUP

If cooking pumpkins are out of season, try making this soup with butternut, acorn, or any winter squash. The soup can be served warm as great way to start a winter meal or chilled for a summer luncheon. The light curry flavor, the smooth texture, and the crunchy pumpkin seeds add up to a dish that could be served at an elegant party or dinner for your family.

SERVES 8

1¹/₂ TABLESPOONS BUTTER

³/₄ CUP DICED ONION

6 CUPS PEELED, SEEDED, AND DICED PUMPKIN

1 TEASPOON CHOPPED GARLIC

1¹/₂ TEASPOONS CURRY POWDER

2 TABLESPOONS FLOUR

5 CUPS CHICKEN STOCK

SALT AND PEPPER

¹/₂ CUP WHIPPING CREAM

¹/₄ CUP TOASTED PUMPKIN SEEDS (PEPITAS), OR CROUTONS (OPTIONAL)

PLACE THE BUTTER and onion in a large pot and cook over medium heat for 10 minutes, or until the onions are translucent. Add the pumpkin and cook for 5 minutes. Sprinkle the garlic, curry powder, and flour over the pumpkin and toss until evenly mixed. Slowly pour in the chicken stock and bring to a boil. Simmer for 15 minutes, or until the pumpkin is very soft. Purée the soup until smooth. Season to taste with salt and pepper and stir in the cream.

LADLE THE SOUP into bowls and sprinkle with the pumpkin seeds.

🍇 WINE SUGGESTION: Semisweet white wine

EGG DROP SOUP

I call this "Oh Shoot Soup" (or something like that). In other words, "Oh shoot, I forgot to make the soup." This goes together in a snap and you can use any vegetables you have on hand at the time with great results.

SERVES 8

½ CUP DICED RED ONION

3 TABLESPOONS SLIVERED GARLIC

2 TABLESPOONS MINCED GINGER

¾ CUP SLICED SHIITAKE MUSHROOMS

½ CUP DRIED PADI STRAW MUSHROOMS, RECONSTITUTED

½ STALK CELERY, SLICED ON THE DIAGONAL

2 TABLESPOONS SESAME OIL

¼ CUP PEANUT OIL

2 QUARTS CHICKEN STOCK

PINCH OF CHINESE FIVE SPICE

½ TEASPOON RED PEPPER FLAKES

¾ CUP WOOD EAR MUSHROOMS, REHYDRATED AND JULIENNED

3 TABLESPOONS CORNSTARCH

½ CUP SOY SAUCE

½ CUP JULIENNED CARROT

¼ CUP JULIENNED RED BELL PEPPER

¾ CUP SHREDDED NAPA CABBAGE

¾ CUP SHREDDED BOK CHOY

¼ CUP SLICED WATER CHESTNUTS

1 TABLESPOON CHOPPED NORI

2 EGGS, LIGHTLY WHISKED

SALT AND WHITE PEPPER

4 GREEN ONIONS, SLICED ON THE DIAGONAL

SAUTÉ THE RED ONION, garlic, ginger, shiitake and straw mushrooms, and celery in the sesame and peanut oils over medium-high heat for 5 minutes, or until the onions are tender. Add the stock, Chinese five spice, red pepper flakes, and wood ear mushrooms and bring to a boil.

COMBINE THE CORNSTARCH and soy sauce to make a slurry. Stir the slurry into the simmering soup and bring back to a boil. Add the carrots, red bell pepper, Napa cabbage, bok choy, water chestnuts, and nori and bring to a rolling boil. Slowly pour in the whisked eggs, stirring very gently, and simmer for 2 minutes. Season to taste with salt and white pepper, ladle into bowls, and garnish with the green onions.

🍇 WINE SUGGESTION: Fruity red wine

PEACH-LAVENDER SOUP

Although this is a slightly sweet soup, I think the combination of flavors makes a light, refreshing starter for a summer meal. I like to make my own crème fraîche for this soup. It is easy to make by adding 2 tablespoons of buttermilk to 1 cup of whipping cream and letting it stand at room temperature for 8 to 24 hours, or until it is very thick. It can then be refrigerated for up to 10 days.

SERVES 6

1 TABLESPOON PLUS 1 TEASPOON CHOPPED FRESH LAVENDER FLOWERS

1 CUP SUGAR

1/4 CUP WATER

10 MEDIUM PEACHES, PEELED AND PITTED

1/4 CUP FRESHLY SQUEEZED LEMON JUICE

1/4 CUP AMARETTO

1/2 CUP CRÈME FRAÎCHE

1/4 CUP ROUGHLY CHOPPED TOASTED ALMONDS

PLACE 1 TEASPOON of the lavender, the sugar, and water in small saucepan and bring to a boil. Simmer for 10 minutes, remove from the heat, and cool to room temperature.

CUT THE PEACHES in chunks and purée with the lemon juice, amaretto, and the lavender syrup until smooth. (Superfine sugar may be added if the fruit is not sweet enough.)

LADLE THE SOUP into chilled bowls and top with a dollop of the crème fraîche. Arrange the almonds on the crème fraîche and sprinkle with the remaining 1 tablespoon of lavender.

🍇 WINE SUGGESTION: Semisweet white wine

PACIFIC OYSTER BISQUE

This dish fulfills my 3 R's of cooking: really easy, really impressive, and, most importantly, really good. Even if you aren't a professional oyster shucker, you can put this dish together in less than 30 minutes. If you don't want to shuck your own oysters, you can often find fresh-packed raw oysters in the seafood section of the supermarket.

SERVES 4

- ¼ CUP MINCED SHALLOTS
- 1 SLICE BACON, CHOPPED
- 3 TABLESPOONS BUTTER
- 1 TEASPOON MINCED GARLIC
- 18 PACIFIC OYSTERS, SHUCKED, JUICE RESERVED
- PINCH OF DRIED OREGANO (OR ¼ TEASPOON FRESH OREGANO)

- PINCH OF THYME (OR ¼ TEASPOON FRESH THYME)
- ½ CUP CHARDONNAY
- 2 CUPS WHIPPING CREAM
- 2 CUPS HALF-AND-HALF
- SALT AND PEPPER
- TABASCO SAUCE (OPTIONAL)

SAUTÉ THE SHALLOTS and bacon in the butter in a heavy-bottomed pot over medium heat for 2 minutes. Add the garlic and cook for 1 minute. Add the oysters and their juice, oregano, thyme, and wine and bring to boil. Remove 4 of the oysters with a slotted spoon and reserve for garnish. Using a whisk, break up the remaining oysters into smaller pieces. Add the cream and half-and-half, bring to a boil, and simmer for 5 minutes. Remove from the heat and season to taste with salt and pepper.

LADLE THE BISQUE into 4 shallow bowls, top with the reserved oysters, and sprinkle with a little Tabasco sauce, if desired.

🍇 WINE SUGGESTION: Crisp or barrel-fermented white wine

OBSESSION SPAGHETTI SQUASH SALAD

This simple salad can be prepared several days ahead and tossed together just before serving. The fresh flavors and the beautiful colors make this perfect for a barbecue or family picnic.

1 MEDIUM SPAGHETTI SQUASH

1 GREEN ONION, MINCED

$1/3$ CUP FRESHLY SQUEEZED ORANGE JUICE

1 TEASPOON MINCED GARLIC

1 TEASPOON MINCED SHALLOT

1 TEASPOON MINCED GINGER

$1^{1}/_{2}$ TABLESPOONS SOY SAUCE

2 TEASPOONS HONEY

3 TABLESPOONS IRONSTONE OBSESSION SYMPHONY

$1^{1}/_{2}$ TABLESPOONS RICE WINE VINEGAR

$1/3$ CUP EXTRA VIRGIN OLIVE OIL

SALT AND PEPPER

$1^{1}/_{2}$ CUPS BROCCOLI FLORETS, BLANCHED AND SHOCKED

ZEST OF 1 ORANGE

1 CUP TOASTED PECAN HALVES

PREHEAT THE OVEN to 350°. Pierce the skin of the squash in several places with a fork and place on a baking sheet. Bake for 30 minutes, turn over, and bake for 30 minutes, or until slightly soft. Cool, cut in half, and remove the seeds. Scrape the flesh into a mixing bowl and fluff with a fork. Refrigerate for 1 hour, or until thoroughly chilled.

COMBINE THE GREEN ONION, orange juice, garlic, shallot, ginger, soy sauce, honey, wine, and vinegar in a bowl and slowly whisk in the olive oil. Season to taste with salt and pepper and refrigerate for 30 minutes, or until chilled.

TOSS THE SQUASH and broccoli with the vinaigrette and place on a serving platter. Sprinkle the orange zest and pecans over the squash.

WINE SUGGESTION: Semisweet white wine

GAZPACHO SALAD

This dish has all of the elements of gazpacho, but they are assembled individually. It can be served as a salad course or as a vegetable tray on a buffet. You can use the recipe as a guide, but any combination of fresh vegetables will be successful with this delicious sun-dried tomato vinaigrette.

SERVES 4

2 TABLESPOONS RED WINE VINEGAR

2 TABLESPOONS FRESHLY SQUEEZED LIME JUICE

1/2 CUP SUN-DRIED TOMATOES, REHYDRATED IN WATER

2 GARLIC CLOVES

PINCH OF CAYENNE PEPPER

1/2 CUP EXTRA VIRGIN OLIVE OIL

1 TABLESPOON CHOPPED FRESH OREGANO

SALT AND PEPPER

3 CUPS MIXED SPRING GREENS

8 BABY CARROTS, PEELED AND GREENS TRIMMED

4 ASSORTED BABY BEETS, PEELED AND HALVED

1 CUCUMBER, CUT IN WEDGES LENGTHWISE

4 JINGLE BELL PEPPERS, HALVED AND SEEDED

1 HEART OF CELERY

1/4 CUP PEA SHOOTS

1/2 CUP CHILI CROUTONS (RECIPE FOLLOWS)

PLACE THE VINEGAR, lime juice, sun-dried tomatoes, garlic, and cayenne pepper in a blender and purée for 20 seconds, or until slightly chunky. Whisk in the olive oil until completely incorporated. Stir in the oregano and season to taste with salt and pepper.

PLACE THE GREENS in the center of a serving platter. Pour the vinaigrette into a small cup and place next to the greens. Arrange the carrots, beets, cucumber, peppers, celery, and pea shoots around the greens and sprinkle with the croutons.

WINE SUGGESTION: Medium-bodied red wine

Chili Croutons
MAKES 2 CUPS

1 JALAPEÑO, SEEDED AND FINELY DICED

1/4 CUP BUTTER

1 TEASPOON FINELY CHOPPED GARLIC

2 CUPS CUBED DAY-OLD FRENCH BREAD

1/4 TEASPOON CHILI POWDER

PREHEAT THE OVEN to 350°. Sauté the jalapeño in the butter over medium heat for 5 minutes, or until soft but not brown. Add the garlic and remove from the heat. Add the bread and chili powder and toss well. Spread the bread cubes in a single layer on a baking sheet and bake for 10 minutes, or to the desired crispness.

SOUTHWESTERN CAESAR SALAD

This salad is a slight twist on a traditional Caesar. Instead of anchovy, I use chili powder in the dressing and the croutons to give the salad a little punch. It is a great way to wake up your taste buds before serving the Chili-Citrus Steak with Chili-Roasted Potatoes (page 124).

SERVES 4

- 2 TABLESPOONS CHILI POWDER
- 2 EGG YOLKS
- 1 TABLESPOON SHERRY VINEGAR
- 2 TABLESPOONS FRESHLY SQUEEZED LEMON JUICE
- 3 GARLIC CLOVES, MINCED

- 1 CUP EXTRA VIRGIN OLIVE OIL
- SALT AND PEPPER
- 1 HEAD ROMAINE LETTUCE, CHOPPED
- 1 CUP CHILI CROUTONS (SEE PAGE 62)
- 1/3 CUP GRATED ROMANO CHEESE

COMBINE THE CHILI POWDER, egg yolks, vinegar, lemon juice, and garlic in a large bowl. Slowly whisk in the olive oil and season to taste with salt and pepper. Cover and refrigerate for 30 minutes, or until chilled.

PLACE THE ROMAINE LETTUCE, Chili Croutons, and grated Romano in a large bowl and toss with the dressing.

WINE SUGGESTION: Light and fruity or crisp white wine

WATERMELON AND JICAMA SALAD

Jicama (pronounced HEE-kah-mah) is a root vegetable that is often referred to as a "Mexican potato". It has a thin brown skin and white flesh that is good both raw and cooked. Its water chestnut—like texture and slightly nutty flavor pair perfectly with the watermelon in this refreshing salad.

SERVES 10

- 1 SEEDLESS WATERMELON
- 2 JICAMAS
- JUICE OF 3 LIMES

- 1/4 CUP CHOPPED CILANTRO
- 1 TABLESPOON CHOPPED MINT
- 1/2 TEASPOON CHILI POWDER

CUT THE WATERMELON into 1-inch cubes, discarding the rind. Refrigerate for 1 hour, or until chilled. Peel the jicama and cut into 1/4- by 2-inch sticks. Refrigerate for 30 minutes, or until chilled.

TOSS TOGETHER THE WATERMELON, jicama, lime juice, cilantro, mint, and chili powder just prior to serving.

WINE SUGGESTION: Semisweet white wine

GRILLED DAY BOAT SCALLOPS
WITH CUCUMBER COUSCOUS
AND LEMON VINAIGRETTE

I am fortunate to be able to get delicious, fresh scallops most of the year. But, if I have to buy frozen, I look for chemical-free, block-frozen scallops. The individually quick-frozen or chemically treated scallops have water added that dilutes the flavor and changes the texture.

SERVES 8

1 CUP ISRAELI COUSCOUS

ZEST OF 2 LEMONS

1/4 CUP FRESHLY SQUEEZED LEMON JUICE

3/4 CUP PEELED, SEEDED, AND CHOPPED CUCUMBER

2 GARLIC CLOVES, MINCED

1/4 CUP SNOW PEAS, BLANCHED AND DICED IN 1/4-INCH PIECES

2 TABLESPOONS JULIENNED BASIL

1/4 CUP EXTRA VIRGIN OLIVE OIL

SALT AND PEPPER

16 LARGE SCALLOPS

24 THIN CUCUMBER SLICES

1/2 CUP CHERVIL SPRIGS

BRING 1 CUP OF SALTED WATER to a boil. Stir in the couscous, cover, and simmer for 5 minutes. Turn off the heat, and let stand, covered, for 15 minutes. Place the couscous in a large bowl, cover, and refrigerate for 1 hour, or until chilled.

ADD HALF THE LEMON ZEST, the lemon juice, chopped cucumber, garlic, snow peas, basil, and olive oil to the couscous and mix well. Season to taste with salt and pepper.

PREHEAT THE GRILL. Grill the scallops for 3 to 4 minutes on each side, or until opaque.

PLACE 3 CUCUMBER SLICES in a triangle in the center of each plate. Press about 2/3 cup of the couscous salad into a ramekin and unmold in the center of the cucumbers. Place 2 of the scallops on the couscous. Sprinkle the remaining lemon zest over the scallops and garnish with the chervil sprigs.

WINE SUGGESTION: Crisp or light and fruity white wine

MINER'S LETTUCE SALAD WITH BLACKBERRY-CABERNET VINAIGRETTE

Miner's lettuce, pea shoots, watercress, and blackberries grow wild in the area around the winery, so this was a natural combination for me. If you don't happen to have wild lettuce growing in your backyard, use mesclun greens or spring mix instead.

SERVES 4

- 1/2 CUP BLACKBERRIES, CRUSHED BY HAND
- 1 TABLESPOON MINCED RED ONION
- 1 SMALL GARLIC CLOVE, MINCED
- 3/4 TEASPOON WHOLE-GRAIN MUSTARD
- 1 TABLESPOON HONEY
- 2 1/2 TABLESPOONS SHERRY VINEGAR
- 1/2 TEASPOON WORCESTERSHIRE SAUCE
- 1 1/2 TEASPOONS WATER
- 1 TABLESPOON CABERNET SAUVIGNON
- 1/4 CUP PLUS 1 TABLESPOON EXTRA VIRGIN OLIVE OIL

- 1 CUP CANOLA OIL
- SALT AND PEPPER
- 4 VERY THIN FRENCH BREAD SLICES, ABOUT 1 1/2 BY 10 INCHES
- 2 YELLOW TOMATOES, THINLY SLICED
- 2 CUPS MINER'S LETTUCE
- 1/2 CUP PEA SHOOTS
- 1/2 CUP WATERCRESS
- 1/2 CUP WHOLE BLACKBERRIES

COMBINE THE CRUSHED BLACKBERRIES, onion, garlic, mustard, honey, vinegar, Worcestershire sauce, water, and wine in a small bowl. Slowly whisk in 1/4 cup of the olive oil and the canola oil. Season to taste with salt and pepper.

PREHEAT THE OVEN to 350°. Brush the bread slices with the remaining 1 tablespoon of olive oil and wrap them around 3-inch ring molds. (Empty soda cans work well.) Bake the bread slices for 5 to 7 minutes, or until golden brown. Let cool and carefully remove the bread from the ring mold.

ARRANGE SOME OF THE TOMATO SLICES in a circle in the center of each plate and top with a bread circle. Combine the miner's lettuce, pea shoots, and watercress and gently place inside the bread circle. Arrange the whole blackberries on the plate and drizzle the vinaigrette over the salad and around the plate.

🍇 WINE SUGGESTION: Full-bodied red wine

Nectarine and Butter Lettuce Salad

This salad tastes like summer. That is the only way to describe the fresh flavor of this nectarine vinaigrette paired with the soft lettuce and sweet-sharp shallots.

Serves 6

2 RIPE NECTARINES

1 TABLESPOON BUTTER

1 TABLESPOON MINCED SHALLOT

1 CUP CHARDONNAY

2 VANILLA BEANS, SPLIT LENGTHWISE

1 TABLESPOON BROWN SUGAR

2 TABLESPOONS WHITE WINE VINEGAR

1/2 TEASPOON BLACK PEPPER

1/4 CUP CANOLA OIL

2 HEADS BUTTER LETTUCE

1 SHALLOT, PEELED AND THINLY SLICED

SPLIT 1 OF THE NECTARINES in half and remove the pit. Sauté the nectarine halves in the butter, split down side, over medium heat for 5 minutes, or until evenly browned. Turn over the nectarine halves and add the minced shallot to the pan. Cook for 1 minute, or until the shallots are tender. Add the wine and vanilla beans and cook for 10 minutes, or until the liquid is reduced to about 1/3 cup.

SCRAPE ANY REMAINING PULP from the vanilla beans into a blender. Add the browned nectarine and wine mixture and purée until smooth. Pour the mixture into a bowl, add the brown sugar, vinegar, and pepper, and slowly whisk in the oil.

CUT THE REMAINING NECTARINE in half and cut each half into 9 slices.

TOSS THE LETTUCE with half of the nectarine vinaigrette and place some in the center of each plate. Fan 3 nectarine slices over the lettuce and top with the sliced shallot. Drizzle the remaining vinaigrette over the salad and sprinkle with pepper.

WINE SUGGESTION: Champagne and sparkling or semisweet white wine

TROPICAL FRUIT with SPICED RUM CRÈME FRAÎCHE

Tropical fruits make a great winter salad. Not only are they at the peak of their season, they help break up the winter doldrums. This combination of spiced rum and tropical fruit never fails to remind me that warmer weather is just around the corner. This salad can be served individually plated, as I have done here, or you can toss the fruit with the crème fraîche and serve family-style.

SERVES 6

1 CUP CRÈME FRAÎCHE (SEE HEADNONTE PAGE 60)

2 TABLESPOONS SPICED RUM

2 MANGOES, PEELED AND SLICED

2 BANANAS, PEELED AND SLICED

1 PINEAPPLE, PEELED, CORED, AND SLICED

2 KIWIS, PEELED AND SLICED

1 LIME, CUT IN 6 WEDGES

6 MINT SPRIGS

1/2 CUP TOASTED, CHOPPED MACADAMIA NUTS

COMBINE THE CRÈME FRAÎCHE and spiced rum in a small bowl and set aside.

ARRANGE THE MANGO, banana, and pineapple slices in wedges to form a circle in the center of each plate. Place the kiwi in the center of the circle and drizzle the crème fraîche over the fruit and around the plate. Place a lime wedge on each plate and garnish with a mint sprig and macadamia nuts.

WINE SUGGESTION: Semisweet white wine

Mediterranean Tuna Salad

I first tried rémoulade sauce when I was working in New Orleans. It seemed to me that when they served seafood they served rémoulade, and I came to think of it as "New Orleans tartar sauce". It is wonderful as a tangy dressing for this salad, but it is also tasty with any type of grilled, boiled, or fried seafood.

Serves 4

4 1/2-INCH-THICK SLICES FRENCH BREAD

3 TABLESPOONS EXTRA VIRGIN OLIVE OIL

SALT AND PEPPER

5 OUNCES SASHIMI-GRADE AHI TUNA

1 TOMATO, THINLY SLICED

RÉMOULADE SAUCE (RECIPE FOLLOWS)

1 SMALL HEAD ROMAINE LETTUCE

2 TABLESPOONS FINELY DICED RED ONION

1 LEMON, CUT IN WEDGES

PREHEAT THE BROILER. Brush the bread slices with 2 tablespoons of the olive oil and sprinkle with salt and pepper. Broil for 2 to 3 minutes, or until golden brown.

SEASON THE TUNA with salt and pepper. Heat the remaining 1 tablespoon of olive oil in a sauté pan and sear the tuna for 2 to 3 minutes on each side, or until still rare in the center. Let rest for 5 minutes and thinly slice.

PLACE A PIECE of toasted bread in the center of each plate and top with some of the tomato slices. Spoon the Rémoulade Sauce next to the bread and arrange the tuna slices over the tomato. Place several lettuce leaves next to the tuna and sprinkle the red onion over the tuna and lettuce. Place a lemon wedge next to the lettuce and serve immediately.

🍇 WINE SUGGESTION: Crisp or barrel-fermented white wine

Rémoulade Sauce
MAKES APPROXIMATELY 1 1/2 CUPS

2 TABLESPOONS MINCED CELERY

2 TABLESPOONS MINCED ONION

2 TABLESPOONS MINCED GREEN PEPPER

1 CUP MAYONNAISE

2 TABLESPOONS WHOLE-GRAIN MUSTARD

1 1/2 TEASPOONS FRESHLY SQUEEZED LEMON JUICE

1 1/2 TEASPOONS CHOPPED GARLIC

1/2 TEASPOON WORCESTERSHIRE SAUCE

1/2 TEASPOON TABASCO SAUCE

1/2 TEASPOON COARSELY GROUND PEPPER

1/4 TEASPOON SALT

PINCH OF PAPRIKA

COMBINE ALL OF THE INGREDIENTS in a small bowl and refrigerate for 1 hour, or until ready to use.

Roasted Chicken Salad with Portobello Mushroom Vinaigrette

This is a great make-ahead dish. All of the ingredients can be prepared up to a day in advance and tossed together at the last minute. Roasting the vegetables and chicken really brings out the flavor of the ingredients and provides a richness and depth that make this a very satisfying salad.

SERVES 6

1 WHOLE CHICKEN (2½ TO 3 POUNDS)

12 THYME SPRIGS

SALT AND PEPPER

4 PORTOBELLO MUSHROOMS, STEMS AND GILLS REMOVED

½ CUP EXTRA VIRGIN OLIVE OIL

1½ CUPS TEARDROP OR SMALL CHERRY TOMATOES

3 TABLESPOONS BALSAMIC VINEGAR

1 RED BELL PEPPER

1 YELLOW BELL PEPPER

2 SUN-DRIED TOMATOES, IN OIL

1 TEASPOON MINCED GARLIC

1 SHALLOT, MINCED

½ TEASPOON WHOLE-GRAIN MUSTARD

6 CUPS MESCLUN GREENS

PREHEAT THE OVEN to 350°. Rinse the chicken under cool water and place in a baking pan. Place 10 of the thyme sprigs in the cavity of the chicken and season inside and out with salt and pepper. Roast for 1 hour, or until the juices from the thigh run clear. Remove from the oven and cool to room temperature. Remove the chicken from the bones and cut into ¼-inch-thick slices.

DICE THE PORTOBELLOS into ½-inch pieces and place on a shallow baking pan. Toss the mushrooms with 1 tablespoon of the olive oil and season with salt and pepper. Roast for 15 minutes, remove from the oven, and set aside.

PLACE THE TOMATOES in a small baking dish with the remaining 7 tablespoons of olive oil, the remaining 2 thyme sprigs, and the balsamic vinegar. Cover tightly with aluminum foil and roast for 15 minutes, or until the tomatoes just begin to pop open. Remove from the oven and reserve the tomatoes and liquid separately.

ROAST THE WHOLE RED and yellow bell peppers on the stovetop flame or under the broiler for 10 minutes, or until completely black on all sides. Immediately place the peppers in a bowl and cover tightly with plastic wrap. Let stand for 10 minutes then peel off the charred skin. Remove the stems and seeds from the peppers and dice into $^{1}/_{2}$-inch pieces.

PLACE HALF OF THE MUSHROOMS in a food processor with the sun-dried tomatoes and purée until smooth. Add the garlic, shallot, and mustard and pulse the processor while slowly adding the liquid from the roasted tomatoes. Season to taste with salt and pepper.

TOSS THE MESCLUN GREENS with half of the vinaigrette and place some of the greens in the center of each plate. Sprinkle the roasted red and yellow bell pepper pieces, the remaining mushrooms, and the tomatoes over the greens. Arrange the chicken slices on top of the greens and drizzle the remaining vinaigrette over the chicken and greens.

WINE SUGGESTION: Medium-bodied red wine

ENTRÉES

PANCETTA-WRAPPED SEA SCALLOPS WITH HERB RISOTTO

I call this comfort food goes upscale because the elegant look belies the rich, hearty flavors and textures of this extremely satisfying dish. I have adjusted the traditional method of making risotto. The result is the same creamy texture without having to stand over the pan and stir constantly.

SERVES 4

- 1 1/2 CUPS FINELY DICED ONION
- 3/4 CUP BUTTER, AT ROOM TEMPERATURE
- 1 1/4 TEASPOONS MINCED GARLIC
- 1 TEASPOON FRESH THYME LEAVES
- 1 TEASPOON KOSHER SALT
- 2 CUPS ARBORIO RICE
- 8 CUPS CLAM JUICE
- 12 LARGE SEA SCALLOPS
- 12 SLICES PANCETTA

- SALT AND PEPPER
- FLOUR FOR DUSTING
- 1/2 TEASPOON CHOPPED FRESH THYME
- 1/4 CUP CHARDONNAY
- 2 TABLESPOONS FRESHLY SQUEEZED LEMON JUICE
- 1/2 CUP WHIPPING CREAM
- 4 THYME SPRIGS

SAUTÉ THE ONION in 1/2 cup of the butter in a large skillet for 10 minutes, or until soft. Stir in 1 teaspoon of the garlic, the thyme leaves, and salt. Add the rice and stir until completely coated with butter. Stir in the clam juice and bring to a boil. Simmer uncovered, stirring frequently, for 40 minutes, or until the rice is cooked and the liquid has been absorbed. Keep warm until ready to serve.

PREHEAT THE OVEN to 400°. Pat the scallops dry with a paper towel. Wrap 1 pancetta slice around each scallop, leaving the flat ends exposed. Season the scallops with salt and pepper and lightly dust the exposed ends with the flour.

PLACE 1 TABLESPOON of the butter in an oven-proof sauté pan and melt over medium-high heat. Add the scallops and cook for 2 minutes. Turn the scallops over and then place the pan in the oven for 2 to 3 minutes, or until the scallops are opaque. Remove the scallops from the pan and keep warm.

PLACE THE REMAINING 1/4 teaspoon of garlic in the pan and cook over medium-high heat for 30 seconds. Add the chopped thyme, wine, and lemon juice and cook for 2 to 3 minutes, or until reduced to about 1/4 cup. Add the cream and cook for 3 to 5 minutes, or until reduced to a scant 1/2 cup. Remove from the heat and slowly stir in the remaining 3 tablespoons of butter. Season to taste with salt and pepper. Stir one half of the sauce into the risotto.

SPOON SOME OF THE RISOTTO in the center of each plate and top with 3 of the scallops. Drizzle the remaining sauce over the scallops and garnish with the thyme sprigs.

🍇 WINE SUGGESTION: Barrel-fermented white wine

BARBECUED LOBSTER TAILS
WITH HEARTS OF ROMAINE

The first time I served this dish was for a barbecue on a white-water rafting trip. I was trying to come up with a way to cook a nice dinner while camping, and what could be more perfect than barbecued lobster? I think that serving the lobsters in such a casual way actually makes them seem even more decadent.

SERVES 4

6 SLICES DAY-OLD FRENCH BREAD

3 TABLESPOONS MELTED BUTTER

1/4 TEASPOON CHILI POWDER

1 CUP BUTTER

2 TABLESPOONS CHOPPED SHALLOT

2 TABLESPOONS CHOPPED GARLIC

3/4 CUP CHARDONNAY

1/4 CUP FRESHLY SQUEEZED LEMON JUICE

1/4 CUP WHOLE-GRAIN MUSTARD

1 1/2 TABLESPOONS WORCESTERSHIRE SAUCE

2 TEASPOONS TABASCO SAUCE

1 TABLESPOON FRESH ROSEMARY LEAVES

1 1/2 TEASPOONS BLACK PEPPER

SALT

4 LOBSTER TAILS, SHELLS REMOVED
   (6 TO 8 OUNCES EACH)

2 TABLESPOONS EXTRA VIRGIN OLIVE OIL

4 ROMAINE HEARTS, QUARTERED

1 LIME, CUT IN WEDGES

PREHEAT THE OVEN to 350°. Cut 2 of the bread slices into bite-sized cubes. Brush the 4 remaining bread slices with some of the melted butter and toss the cubes with the remaining melted butter. Place the bread slices and cubes in a single layer on a baking sheet and sprinkle with the chili powder. Bake for 10 minutes, or until golden brown.

PREHEAT THE GRILL. Combine the butter, shallot, garlic, wine, lemon juice, mustard, Worcestershire sauce, Tabasco sauce, rosemary, and pepper in a saucepan. Bring to a boil over high heat, reduce to medium-low heat, and simmer until the butter is completely melted. Season to taste with salt and keep warm until ready to use.

BRUSH THE LOBSTER TAILS with the sauce and grill for 3 to 4 minutes on each side, or until opaque.

HEAT THE OLIVE OIL in a large sauté pan, add the romaine hearts, and cook for 2 minutes, or until lightly wilted.

ARRANGE THE ROMAINE QUARTERS on one side of each plate. Place a toasted bread slice next to the romaine and top with a lobster tail. Drizzle the remaining sauce over the lobster and romaine. Sprinkle the croutons over the lettuce and garnish with the lime wedges.

🍇 WINE SUGGESTION: Crisp white wine

SAND DABS WITH SAVORY GRITS

Sand dabs are a small fish similar to sole in flavor and texture. They are prevalent around the sandy bay areas of the central Pacific coast. Growing up in Monterey, I would often go salmon fishing, but if the salmon weren't biting, I would head in toward the beach and fish for sand dabs. They are a great treat, but if you can't get them, fillet of sole is a good substitute.

SERVES 4

1 ARTICHOKE	3 CUPS CHICKEN STOCK
1/2 CUP MILK	1 CUP HALF-AND-HALF
1 LEMON, THINLY SLICED	1 TEASPOON SALT
1 SMALL FENNEL BULB, THINLY SLICED	1 TABLESPOON CHOPPED FRESH TARRAGON
1/2 CUP FLOUR	1/2 CUP DICED ARTICHOKE BOTTOMS, COOKED
VEGETABLE OIL FOR DEEP FRYING	1/4 CUP FRESHLY SQUEEZED LEMON JUICE
SALT AND PEPPER	1/4 CUP WHITE WINE
1/2 CUP FINELY DICED ONION	3 TABLESPOONS OLIVE OIL
6 TABLESPOONS PLUS 1 TEASPOON BUTTER	1 CUP CRACKER MEAL
1 TEASPOON MINCED GARLIC	2 TABLESPOONS GRANULATED GARLIC
1 1/2 CUPS GRITS	8 SAND DAB FILETS

PREHEAT THE OIL to 350°. Remove the leaves and choke from the artichoke and peel the bottom. Cut the artichoke bottom into thin slices and immediately place them in the milk. Drain the milk and dust the artichoke, lemon, and fennel slices with the flour. Fry the slices in the oil for 3 to 5 minutes, or until golden brown. Drain on paper towels and immediately season with salt and pepper.

PLACE THE ONION and 2 tablespoons of the butter in a saucepan and cook over medium heat for 10 minutes, or until tender. Add 1/2 teaspoon of garlic and cook for 1 minute. Add the grits and stir until completely coated with the butter. Add the chicken stock, half-and-half, and salt, cover, and simmer over medium-low heat, stirring occasionally, for 15 minutes, or until tender. Stir in the tarragon, artichoke bottoms, 2 tablespoon of the butter, the remaining 1/2 teaspoon garlic, 2 tablespoons of the lemon juice and 2 tablespoons of the wine and remove from the heat.

HEAT THE OLIVE OIL and 1 teaspoon of the butter in a large sauté pan. Combine the cracker meal and granulated garlic in a shallow bowl. Dredge the sand dabs in the cracker meal and sauté for 2 to 3 minutes on each side, or until golden brown.

HEAT THE REMAINING 2 tablespoons of butter in a saucepan for 3 minutes, or until browned. Remove from the heat and whisk in the remaining 2 tablespoons of wine and 2 tablespoons of lemon juice.

SPOON SOME OF THE GRITS into each shallow bowl. Spoon some of the sauce over the grits and top with the sand dabs. Arrange the fried lemon slices, artichokes and fennel over the sand dabs.

🍇 WINE SUGGESTION: Barrel-fermented or light and fruity white wine

QUICK SPICY CIOPPINO

The key to this dish is to not overcook the seafood. As soon as is starts to boil, get the pan off the heat. Cooking the seafood in the shells makes it a little messy to eat, but it tastes much better. And besides, you can't be afraid of a little mess when you're talking about cioppino.

SERVES 10

- 4 CANS (26 OUNCE) WHOLE PEAR TOMATOES, CRUSHED BY HAND
- 1/4 CUP CHOPPED GARLIC
- 2 TABLESPOONS DRIED BASIL
- 1 TABLESPOON DRIED OREGANO
- 2 TABLESPOONS CHOPPED SHALLOTS
- 1/2 CUP CHOPPED SUN-DRIED TOMATOES
- 1/4 CUP KALAMATA OLIVES, PITTED AND QUARTERED
- 2 TABLESPOONS CHOPPED ANCHOVY FILLETS
- 1/4 TEASPOON RED PEPPER FLAKES

- 1/2 CUP PLUS 2 TABLESPOONS EXTRA VIRGIN OLIVE OIL
- 1 CUP ZINFANDEL
- 20 JUMBO PRAWNS, SHELL ON
- 30 SMALL CLAMS, CLEANED
- 30 MUSSELS, CLEANED AND DEBEARDED
- 30 CRAB CLAWS
- 1 1/2 POUNDS WHITE FISH (HALIBUT, SEA BASS, SNAPPER, ETC.), CUT IN 1-INCH CHUNKS
- 1 BAGUETTE FRENCH BREAD, SLICED 1 1/2 THICK
- 1 TABLESPOON FINELY CHOPPED FRESH BASIL

PLACE THE TOMATOES, garlic, dried basil, oregano, shallots, sun-dried tomatoes, olives, anchovies, and red pepper flakes in a bowl. Cook 1/2 cup of the olive oil in a large pot over high heat until it just begins to smoke. Add the tomato mixture to the pan and bring to a boil. Add the wine, reduce to medium-low heat, and simmer for 20 minutes. Gently stir in the prawns, clams, mussels, crab claws, and fish. Increase the heat to high, bring to a boil, and immediately remove from the heat.

PREHEAT THE OVEN to 400°. Brush the bread with the remaining 2 tablespoons of olive oil and sprinkle with the basil. Place on a sheet pan and toast in the oven for 5 to 7 minutes, or until light golden brown.

SPOON THE CIOPPINO into individual terrines and serve with the bread slices on the side.

🍇 WINE SUGGESTION: Medium-bodied red wine

SICILIAN CRAB

This is not a dish to serve at an elegant dinner party. Getting to all of the delicious crabmeat can be a little messy, but is well worth it. So serve it up with lots of crusty sourdough bread to dip in the sauce and plenty of napkins.

SERVES 4

2 TABLESPOONS CHOPPED GARLIC

2 TABLESPOONS CHOPPED SHALLOT

1/4 CUP EXTRA VIRGIN OLIVE OIL

3 DUNGENESS CRABS, COOKED, CRACKED, AND
    CLEANED

4 CUPS CANNED DICED TOMATOES WITH JUICE

1/2 CUP CHARDONNAY

1/2 CUP FISH STOCK OR CLAM JUICE

1 TEASPOON RED PEPPER FLAKES

1/2 CUP BUTTER

1/2 CUP COARSELY CHOPPED BASIL

1/2 CUP FRESHLY SQUEEZED LEMON JUICE

1/4 CUP CHOPPED PARSLEY

SALT AND PEPPER

PLACE THE GARLIC, shallot, and olive oil in a large sauté pan over high heat and cook for 1 minute. Add the crab, tomatoes, wine, stock, red pepper flakes, and butter.

COVER THE PAN and simmer for 5 minutes. Add the basil, lemon juice, and parsley and cook for 2 minutes. Season to taste with salt and pepper and serve in the pan or in a large pasta bowl.

WINE SUGGESTION: Crisp white wine

MEDITERRANEAN BAKED HALIBUT

Need an impressive meal in a hurry? Here's one that's really simple and really good! This dish can be prepared with any type of whitefish and just about any combination of peppers, olives, and vegetables that you can find in your refrigerator.

SERVES 8

2 GARLIC CLOVES, SLIVERED

1/2 CUP JULIENNED ROASTED RED BELL
   PEPPER

15 CAPERBERRIES OR CAPERS

1/4 CUP KALAMATA OLIVES, PITTED AND
   QUARTERED

1 TABLESPOON BALSAMIC VINEGAR

1 TEASPOON FRESH THYME

1 CUP QUARTERED ARTICHOKE HEARTS

1/2 CUP SLICED PEPPERONCINI

1/4 CUP COARSELY CHOPPED BASIL

1 TABLESPOON BLACK PEPPER

1/4 CUP OLIVE OIL

3-POUND HALIBUT FILLET, BONED AND SKINNED

SALT AND PEPPER

PREHEAT THE OVEN TO 400°. Combine the garlic, red bell pepper, caperberries, olives, balsamic vinegar, thyme, artichoke hearts, pepperoncini, basil, pepper, and olive oil in a bowl.

RINSE THE HALIBUT AND PAT DRY. Season with salt and pepper and place in an oiled baking pan. Spoon the olive mixture over the halibut and bake for 12 to 15 minutes, or until the fish is opaque. Remove from the oven and let rest for 5 minutes before serving.

🍇 WINE SUGGESTION: Barrel-fermented white wine

SEAFOOD TURNOVER
WITH CHIVE BEURRE BLANC

If I believed in signature dishes, this would probably be mine. The blend of flavors and textures make this simple yet elegant dish very popular at the winery. Here I have used salmon and scallops, but almost any combination of seafood would work well.

SERVES 4

- 1/2 CUP CHOPPED LEEK
- 1 TABLESPOON PLUS 1 TEASPOON BUTTER, AT ROOM TEMPERATURE
- 3/4 CUP WHIPPING CREAM
- 2 TEASPOONS ROMANO CHEESE
- 1/4 TEASPOON MINCED GARLIC
- 1 PUFF PASTRY SHEET, CUT IN 4 SQUARES

- 4 OUNCES DUNGENESS CRABMEAT
- 1/2-POUND SALMON FILLET, CUT IN 8 PIECES
- 8 SCALLOPS
- 1 TEASPOON CHOPPED SHALLOT
- 1/2 CUP WHITE VINEGAR
- SALT AND PEPPER
- 1 TABLESPOON CHOPPED CHIVES

SAUTÉ THE LEEK in 1 teaspoon of the butter over medium heat for 5 minutes, or until soft but not brown. Add 1/4 cup of the cream, the Romano cheese, and garlic and cook for 5 minutes, or until thickened.

PREHEAT THE OVEN to 375°. Place one tablespoon of the leeks in the center of each pastry square and top with the crabmeat. Place a piece of salmon on 2 sides of each pastry square along the center of the outside edge. Place a scallop on the remaining 2 sides of each pastry square. Fold the corners of the squares into the center and pinch together. (The top of the salmon and scallops will be visible.) Place the turnovers on a parchment-lined baking sheet and bake for 10 to 15 minutes, or until golden brown.

SIMMER THE SHALLOT and vinegar over medium-high heat for 5 minutes, or until almost dry. Add the remaining 1/2 cup cream and cook for 10 minutes, or until reduced to about 1/3 cup. Remove from the heat and stir in the remaining 1 tablespoon of butter. Season to taste with salt and pepper and add the chives just prior to serving.

SPOON SOME OF THE SAUCE into the center of each plate and top with a turnover.

WINE SUGGESTION: Barrel-fermented white wine

Scotch and Dill Salmon with Peppercorn Crust

The smoky peat flavors of the Scotch really showcase the peppercorn crust on the salmon in this dish. But don't worry, there will be plenty of Scotch left to enjoy after dinner with a nice cigar.

Serves 6

- 1/4 CUP FINELY CHOPPED ONION
- 1/2 CUP BUTTER, ROOM TEMPERATURE
- 1 CUP WHITE RICE
- 1 TEASPOON DRIED DILL
- 1 3/4 CUPS CHICKEN STOCK
- 6 SALMON FILLETS (APPROXIMATELY 6 OUNCES EACH)
- 1/4 CUP TRICOLOR PEPPERCORNS, COARSELY GROUND
- 1/4 CUP EXTRA VIRGIN OLIVE OIL

- 1 RED ONION, JULIENNED
- 2 TABLESPOONS CHOPPED GARLIC
- 1 TEASPOON FLOUR
- 1/4 CUP PLUS 1 TABLESPOON SCOTCH
- 1/2 CUP WHITE WINE
- 1/2 CUP FISH STOCK OR CLAM JUICE
- 1 TEASPOON CHOPPED FRESH DILL
- KOSHER SALT
- 6 DILL SPRIGS

SAUTÉ THE ONION in 2 tablespoons of the butter for 5 minutes, or until soft. Add the rice and dried dill and stir well. Add the chicken stock, cover, and simmer for 20 to 25 minutes, or until the rice is tender.

PREHEAT THE OVEN to 400°. Heat an ovenproof skillet over medium-high heat. Coat the top of the salmon fillets with the ground peppercorns. Place the olive oil in the skillet and add the salmon fillets, pepper side down. Cook for 3 to 4 minutes, or until browned. Turn over the salmon, place the skillet into the oven, and cook for 5 minutes. Remove the salmon from the skillet and keep warm.

PLACE THE RED ONION in the skillet and cook for 5 minutes, or until it just starts to brown. Add the garlic and flour and cook, stirring constantly, for 1 minute. Remove the pan from the flame, add 1/4 cup of the Scotch, and return the pan to the stove. Add the white wine and simmer for 2 minutes. Add the fish stock and chopped dill to the pan and simmer for 2 minutes. Remove the skillet from the heat, add the remaining 6 tablespoons of butter, and stir until fully incorporated. Stir in the remaining 1 tablespoon Scotch and season to taste with kosher salt.

PLACE SOME OF THE RICE in the center of each plate and top with a salmon fillet. Spoon the sauce over the salmon and around the plate and garnish with the dill sprigs.

WINE SUGGESTION: Barrel-fermented white wine

WHOLE GRILLED SALMON

This is a great dish for a casual party or barbecue. The lemon, butter, garlic, and dill baste the salmon as it cooks, resulting in a moist, melt-in-your-mouth texture and a delicious, subtle flavor. I like to serve the whole fish on a platter, peel back the skin, and let my guests have at it.

SERVES 8

1 WHOLE SALMON (6 TO 9 POUNDS)

5 LEMONS

6 GARLIC CLOVES, THINLY SLICED

4 DILL SPRIGS

1/2 CUP BUTTER

1/2 CUP EXTRA VIRGIN OLIVE OIL

SALT AND PEPPER

PREHEAT THE GRILL. Rinse the salmon with cold water, making sure the belly cavity is clean. Make small, deep cuts about every fifth bone in the cavity on both sides of the backbone, being careful not to cut through the skin.

CUT 1 OF THE LEMONS into very thin wedges. Insert a slice of garlic, a lemon wedge, a small piece of dill, and a small piece of butter into each of the cuts. Rub the fish inside and out with the olive oil and season with salt and pepper.

GRILL THE SALMON for 10 minutes, roll the salmon over, and grill for 10 to 15 minutes longer, or until just cooked through.

PLACE THE SALMON on a serving platter. Cut the remaining 4 lemons into wedges and arrange them around the salmon.

WINE SUGGESTION: Crisp white wine

PASTA WITH ITALIAN SAUSAGE AND ZINFANDEL MUSHROOMS

The classic pairing of fresh tomatoes and Zinfandel give this dish a depth of flavor that that doesn't seem possible in a meal that can be prepared in less than 30 minutes. I like to slice the garlic for this dish to give it more texture and little pops of garlic flavor.

SERVES 4

- 1/4 CUP EXTRA VIRGIN OLIVE OIL
- 8 OUNCES ITALIAN SAUSAGE (SEE PAGE 33)
- 1/2 SMALL RED ONION, THINLY SLICED
- 12 BUTTON MUSHROOMS, SLICED
- 1/4 CUP DRIED PORCINI MUSHROOMS
- 1 TEASPOON COARSELY GROUND BLACK PEPPER
- 6 GARLIC CLOVES, THINLY SLICED

- 1/2 CUP ZINFANDEL
- 2 RIPE TOMATOES, COARSELY DICED
- 1/4 CUP PACKED, CHOPPED BASIL LEAVES
- 1/2 CUP GRATED ROMANO CHEESE
- SALT AND PEPPER
- 12 OUNCES BOW TIE OR PENNE PASTA, COOKED
- 1/4 CUP COARSELY CHOPPED PARSLEY

HEAT THE OLIVE OIL in a skillet. Add the sausage and cook for 5 minutes, or until browned. Add the onion and cook for 5 minutes, or until soft. Add the button mushrooms, porcini mushrooms, pepper, and garlic and cook for 3 minutes. Add the wine and cook for 2 minutes. Add the tomatoes, stir, and remove from the heat. Add the basil and 1/4 cup of the Romano cheese. Season to taste with salt and pepper and stir in the hot pasta.

SERVE THE PASTA individually or in a large bowl topped with the remaining 1/4 cup of Romano cheese and the parsley.

🍇 WINE SUGGESTION: Medium-bodied red wine

ASPARAGUS AND PENNE WITH LEMON CREAM

Here is the perfect weekday meal. All of the preparation can easily be completed while the pasta cooks and five minutes later, dinner is ready. This dish dispels the popular thought that asparagus doesn't work with wine. The combination of the lemon and cream minimizes the grassiness of the asparagus, making it the perfect complement to a buttery Chardonnay.

SERVES 4

2 TABLESPOONS BUTTER

1/4 CUP MINCED SHALLOTS

20 ASPARAGUS SPEARS, CUT IN 1-INCH PIECES

ZEST OF 2 LEMONS, FINELY CHOPPED

12 OUNCES PENNE PASTA, COOKED

1/4 CUP CHARDONNAY

1 CUP WHIPPING CREAM

1 TEASPOON FRESHLY SQUEEZED LEMON JUICE

1/2 CUP FRESHLY GRATED ROMANO CHEESE

SALT AND PEPPER

MELT THE BUTTER in a large skillet over medium heat. Add the shallots and asparagus and sauté for 1 minute. Add half of the lemon zest, the cooked pasta, and wine and simmer for 1 minute. Add the cream, lemon juice, and 1/4 cup of the Romano cheese and bring to a simmer. Remove from the heat and season to taste with salt and pepper.

SERVE THE PASTA individually or in a large bowl, topped with the remaining 1/4 cup of Romano cheese and the lemon zest.

WINE SUGGESTION: Barrel-fermented white wine

SWEET POTATO GNOCCHI WITH BROWN BUTTER–SAGE PESTO

Is it a yam or a sweet potato? When orange-fleshed sweet potatoes were first introduced, producers wanted to distinguish them from the more traditional, white-fleshed types so they adopted the African word for the sweet potato plant, *nyami* or *yam*. So the answer is, if it is white-fleshed, it is a sweet potato and if it is orange-fleshed it is a sweet potato that is called a "yam". Here I used sweet potatoes, but yams will work equally well.

SERVES 4

1 LARGE SWEET POTATO, PEELED, BOILED, AND MASHED

2 EGGS, BEATEN

1 TO 1 1/2 CUPS FLOUR

1/2 CUP BUTTER

1 GARLIC CLOVE, SLIVERED

1/4 CUP FINELY CHOPPED SAGE

1/2 CUP TOASTED, COARSELY CHOPPED HAZELNUTS

4 SAGE SPRIGS

COMBINE THE SWEET POTATO, eggs, and 3/4 cup of the flour in a bowl. Add up to 3/4 cup more flour, a little at a time, until the dough just stops being sticky. Roll about 1/2 cup of the dough at a time into a 1/2-inch-diameter cigar-shaped roll. Cut the rolls into 1-inch-long gnocchi and place on a lightly floured baking sheet. (If desired, the gnocchi can be covered with plastic wrap and refrigerated for several hours or frozen for up to 1 month.) Cook the gnocchi in boiling salted water for 3 to 4 minutes, or until they float. Gently remove the gnocchi from the pan with a slotted spoon and drain well.

PLACE THE BUTTER IN A LARGE SAUTÉ PAN over medium heat for 5 minutes, or until completely browned. Add the garlic, sage, and hazelnuts and cook for 1 minute. Add the gnocchi to the pan and toss gently until completely coated. Remove from the heat, place into serving bowls, and garnish with the sage sprigs.

🍇 WINE SUGGESTION: Crisp or semisweet white wine

IRONSTONE MACARONI AND CHEESE

Adding three different cheeses and a few herbs makes this everyday dish really stand out. I used Romano, goat, and blue cheese, but almost any combination of cheeses works well. Any type of pasta can be used, so here is your opportunity to use that guitar-shaped pasta that seemed like a good idea when you bought it three years ago!

SERVES 8

- 2 CUPS WHIPPING CREAM
- 1 TABLESPOON CORNSTARCH
- 1/4 CUP FINELY DICED PANCETTA
- 2 TABLESPOONS BUTTER
- 1 TABLESPOON CHOPPED GARLIC
- 1 TEASPOON CHOPPED SHALLOT
- 1/2 TEASPOON OREGANO
- 1 CUP CRUMBLED BLUE CHEESE OR ROQUEFORT
- 1/4 CUP CRUMBLED GOAT CHEESE

- 8 OUNCES PASTA, COOKED
- 1 TABLESPOON MINCED CHIVES
- 1 CUP BREADCRUMBS
- 1 TEASPOON MINCED PARSLEY
- 2 TABLESPOONS FRESHLY GRATED ROMANO CHEESE
- SALT AND PEPPER
- 8 OREGANO SPRIGS

WHISK 1/4 CUP OF THE CREAM with the cornstarch and set aside. Sauté the pancetta in the butter over medium heat for 2 minutes. Add the garlic, shallot, and oregano and cook for 1 minute. Add the blue cheese, goat cheese, and the remaining 1 3/4 cups of cream and bring to a boil. Add the cornstarch mixture to the pan and stir for 5 minutes, or until the sauce thickens. Remove from the heat and stir in the cooked pasta and chives.

PREHEAT THE OVEN to 350°. Place the pasta in individual baking dishes. Combine the breadcrumbs, parsley, Romano cheese, and salt and pepper and sprinkle over the pasta. Bake for 20 minutes, or until browned. (This can also be made family-style by putting it in one large casserole dish and baking for 30 to 40 minutes.) Top each serving with an oregano sprig and serve immediately.

🍇 WINE SUGGESTION: Light and fruity or semisweet white wine

PENNE with SMOKED SALMON and LEEKS

Hot or cold smoked salmon will work equally well in this recipe. Either one will add a smokiness to the sauce that really sets this dish apart. This is a great way to use up any leftover salmon without anyone realizing they are eating those dreaded leftovers.

SERVES 4

1 1/2 CUPS JULIENNED LEEKS

2 TABLESPOONS FINELY CHOPPED SHALLOT

1 TABLESPOON BUTTER

1/4 CUP WHITE WINE

1 CUP WHIPPING CREAM

1/2 CUP DICED SMOKED SALMON

1/2 CUP GRATED ROMANO CHEESE

12 OUNCES PENNE PASTA, COOKED

SALT AND PEPPER

SAUTÉ THE LEEKS and shallot in the butter over medium heat for 3 to 5 minutes, or until soft but not brown. Add the wine and cook for 5 minutes, or until reduced to about 2 tablespoons. Add the cream and bring to a simmer. Stir in the smoked salmon, 1/4 cup of the Romano cheese, and the pasta and bring to a simmer. Cook for 5 minutes, or until it reaches a saucelike consistency. Season to taste with salt and pepper.

PLACE SOME OF THE PASTA in the center of each shallow bowl and sprinkle with the remaining 1/4 cup of Romano cheese.

WINE SUGGESTION: Barrel-fermented white wine

LASAGNA

Bringing the olive oil to the point of smoking before adding the tomatoes cuts their acidity and gives the sauce a great flavor. I'm not a chemist, so I have no idea what chemical reaction causes this, I just know it tastes good. This dish is great for a large group on a busy schedule. It's made a day ahead and only needs to be baked prior to serving.

SERVES 8 TO 10

- 6 TABLESPOONS OLIVE OIL
- 48 OUNCES CANNED WHOLE PEELED TOMATOES, CRUSHED BY HAND
- 2½ TABLESPOONS MINCED GARLIC
- 2 TEASPOONS DRIED BASIL
- ½ TEASPOON DRIED OREGANO
- ¾ TEASPOON RED PEPPER FLAKES
- ½ CUP RED WINE
- 1½ TEASPOONS BALSAMIC VINEGAR
- SALT AND PEPPER

- 1¼ POUNDS ITALIAN SAUSAGE, BROWNED (SEE PAGE 33)
- ½ CUP GRATED CHEDDAR CHEESE
- ½ CUP GRATED JACK CHEESE
- ½ CUP GRATED MOZZARELLA CHEESE
- ½ CUP FRESHLY GRATED ROMANO CHEESE
- 9 LASAGNA NOODLES, UNCOOKED
- 1 BUNCH SPINACH, STEMS REMOVED
- 1½ CUPS RICOTTA CHEESE

PLACE THE OLIVE OIL IN A LARGE POT over high heat and cook for 5 minutes, or until the oil starts to smoke. Add the tomatoes, garlic, basil, oregano, and red pepper flakes to the pan and bring to a boil. Add the wine and balsamic vinegar and simmer for 5 minutes. Season to taste with salt and pepper and remove from the heat. Cool slightly and stir in the Italian sausage.

COMBINE THE CHEDDAR, Jack, mozzarella, and Romano cheeses and set aside. Evenly spread one quarter of the meat sauce in the bottom of a 9- by 13-inch baking pan. Lay 3 of the lasagna noodles in a single layer over the sauce. Ladle one-quarter of the sauce on the pasta and top with one-half of the spinach. Evenly spread one-half of the ricotta cheese over the spinach and sprinkle with one-third of the mixed cheese. Add another layer of noodles, sauce, spinach, ricotta, and mixed cheeses then top with a final layer of pasta, the remaining sauce, and the remaining mixed cheese. Press down on the lasagna to make sure the pasta gets thoroughly coated with the sauce. Cover with plastic wrap and then aluminum foil and refrigerate overnight.

PREHEAT THE OVEN TO 325°. Bake the covered lasagna for 1 hour. (The plastic wrap keeps the tomatoes from reacting to the foil and will not melt on the food.) Remove the aluminum foil and plastic wrap and cook for 15 minutes, or until the cheese is lightly browned. Remove from the oven and let stand for 15 minutes before cutting.

🍇 WINE SUGGESTION: Medium-bodied red wine

IRONSTONE CHICKEN POT PIE

I love this dish after a day skiing or building snowmen with my daughters, Brianna and Haley. It is the ultimate comfort food for those cold winter nights and can be made well ahead of time. You can cook the filling three or four days ahead and just fill your bowls, pop them in the oven until they are hot, and top with pastry at the last minute for a quick winter meal.

SERVES 8

3 MEDIUM TURNIPS, PEELED AND DICED

2 MEDIUM POTATOES, PEELED AND DICED

2 LARGE CARROTS, PEELED AND DICED

12 WILD MUSHROOMS, QUARTERED

2 LARGE ONIONS, DICED

2 GARLIC CLOVES, FINELY CHOPPED

1/4 CUP EXTRA VIRGIN OLIVE OIL

1 WHOLE CHICKEN (3 TO 3 1/2 POUNDS)

SALT AND PEPPER

3/4 CUP FLOUR

5 CUPS CHICKEN STOCK

2 TEASPOONS CHOPPED FRESH ROSEMARY

2 TEASPOONS CHOPPED FRESH PARSLEY

2 TEASPOONS CHOPPED FRESH THYME

1 CUP GREEN PEAS

2 PUFF PASTRY SHEETS

1 EGG, BEATEN

PREHEAT THE OVEN to 350°. Toss the turnips, potatoes, carrots, mushrooms, onions, and garlic in 2 tablespoons of the olive oil in a roasting pan. Rub the chicken with the remaining 2 tablespoons of olive oil, and season with salt and pepper. Place the chicken on top of the vegetables and bake for 45 to 60 minutes, or until the juices from the thigh run clear. (If the vegetables are getting too brown, remove them from the pan and finish cooking the chicken alone.)

REMOVE THE CHICKEN and vegetables from the pan and set aside. Stir the flour into the drippings in the roasting pan and add the chicken stock. Bring to a boil over high heat, reduce to medium heat, and simmer for 10 minutes. Remove from the heat and cool.

CUT THE CHICKEN MEAT into 3/4-inch pieces. Combine the chicken, roasted vegetables, rosemary, parsley, thyme, peas, and sauce in a large saucepan and bring to a simmer. Season to taste with salt and pepper.

PREHEAT THE OVEN to 375°. Cut each puff pastry sheet into 4 squares and place on a parchment-lined baking sheet. Brush the pastry with the egg and bake for 15 minutes, or until the pastry is golden brown.

SPOON THE CHICKEN MIXTURE into 8 bowls and top each with a puff pastry square.

🍷 WINE SUGGESTION: Barrel-fermented white wine

CHICKEN with HERBS and CAPERS

This dish is a great example of how slightly altering the spices will change the wine selection. As it is written, this dish pairs beautifully with Chardonnay, but by adding 1 teaspoon of fresh tarragon to the chicken it leans toward a Cabernet Franc, or adding $1/2$ teaspoon of black pepper would move it to a Cabernet Sauvignon.

SERVES 4

1 CUP WHITE RICE

6 TABLESPOONS BUTTER, AT ROOM TEMPERATURE

1 TEASPOON MINCED GARLIC

1 TEASPOON DRIED TARRAGON

1 TEASPOON DRIED DILL

$1/2$ TEASPOON DRIED BASIL

$1/2$ TEASPOON DRIED OREGANO

3 CUPS CHICKEN STOCK

2 TABLESPOONS EXTRA VIRGIN OLIVE OIL

4 BONELESS, SKINLESS CHICKEN BREASTS, CUT IN $1/2$-INCH-THICK SLICES

SALT AND PEPPER

FLOUR FOR DREDGING

2 TEASPOONS CHOPPED GARLIC

1 TABLESPOON CHOPPED SHALLOT

1 TEASPOON HERBES DE PROVENCE

$1/4$ CUP WHITE WINE

3 TABLESPOONS BALSAMIC VINEGAR

2 TEASPOONS CAPERS

$1/2$ CUP DEMI-GLACE

SAUTÉ THE RICE in 2 tablespoons of the butter for 4 to 5 minutes, or until lightly browned. Add the garlic, tarragon, dill, basil, and oregano and cook for 1 minute. Add the chicken stock, cover, and simmer for 20 to 25 minutes, or until the rice is tender.

HEAT THE OLIVE OIL in a skillet over medium-high heat. Season the chicken with salt and pepper and dredge in the flour, shaking off any excess. Add 1 tablespoon of the butter to the oil and place the chicken in the pan. Cook for 2 minutes, turn over, and cook for 2 minutes more. Stir in the garlic, shallot, and herbes de Provence and cook for 1 minute. Add the wine and balsamic vinegar, reduce to medium-low heat, and cook for 5 minutes. Add the capers and demi-glace and cook for 5 minutes.

Remove from the heat, remove the chicken from the pan, and stir in the remaining 3 tablespoons butter.

SPOON SOME OF THE RICE in the center of each plate. Arrange the chicken slices over the rice and spoon the sauce over the chicken and rice.

WINE SUGGESTION: Light and fruity or semisweet white wine

MERLOT-MARINATED GRILLED QUAIL
WITH YUKON GOLD POTATO CAKES

I developed this dish for a dinner based on the Gold Rush. In my research I found that quail were very prolific in the area during that time and were often eaten by the gold miners. And, of course, I had to include the Yukon Gold potatoes. This dish is also great with Cornish game hens, but do yourself a favor and ask your butcher to bone them for you.

SERVES 4

3/4 CUP MERLOT

3/4 CUP EXTRA VIRGIN OLIVE OIL

1 TABLESPOON SOY SAUCE

1 TABLESPOON BALSAMIC VINEGAR

1 TABLESPOON MINCED GARLIC

2 TABLESPOONS WHOLE-GRAIN MUSTARD

1 1/2 TEASPOONS HONEY

2 TABLESPOONS CHOPPED BASIL

1 1/2 TEASPOONS CHOPPED TARRAGON

SALT AND PEPPER

8 QUAIL, BONED AND HALVED

YUKON GOLD POTATO CAKES (RECIPE FOLLOWS)

COMBINE THE WINE, olive oil, soy sauce, balsamic vinegar, garlic, mustard, honey, basil, and tarragon in a bowl and season with salt and pepper. Add the quail and cover completely with the marinade. Refrigerate for at least 8 hours, or overnight.

PREHEAT THE GRILL. Grill the quail for 2 to 3 minutes on each side, or until done.

PLACE A POTATO CAKE to one side of each plate and arrange 4 quail halves next to the potatoes. Sprinkle with freshly ground pepper and serve immediately.

🍇 WINE SUGGESTION: Light-bodied red wine

Yukon Gold Potato Cakes
MAKES 4 CAKES

1 EGG

1 TABLESPOON MINCED GREEN ONION

1 1/2 TEASPOONS MINCED SHALLOT

2 TABLESPOONS FLOUR

1/2 TEASPOON SALT

1/4 TEASPOON BLACK PEPPER

2 YUKON GOLD POTATOES, PEELED AND THINLY SLICED

2 TABLESPOONS BUTTER

WHISK THE EGG in a large bowl. Stir in the green onion, shallot, flour, salt, and pepper. Add the potatoes and stir until the potato slices are well coated. Preheat the oven to 400°. Cut four 8-inch parchment paper circles and arrange the potato slices in a thin layer on the parchment. Heat an 8-inch nonstick sauté pan over medium-high heat. Melt 1 1/2 teaspoons of butter in the pan and flip 1 of the potato circles into the pan. Remove the parchment paper and sauté for 3 to 4 minutes, or until the potatoes start to brown. Turn over the potatoes and cook for 2 minutes, or until browned.

PLACE THE POTATO CAKE on a baking sheet. Repeat the process with the remaining potatoes. Warm the cakes in the oven for 5 minutes before serving.

DUCK MOUSSAKA

I came up with this dish while preparing for a wine pairing dinner. I needed a dish to go with Zinfandel and thought of moussaka, but since I already had lamb on the menu, I decided to tweak it a little and try it with duck. It was wonderful. This is a great dish for a dinner party. Although it is a little time-consuming to prepare, it can be made up to three days in advance (or frozen for up to one month), and it is guaranteed to impress your guests.

SERVES 6

1 WHOLE DUCK

1 CUP FINELY DICED EGGPLANT

$1/2$ CUP MINCED SHALLOT

2 TABLESPOONS EXTRA VIRGIN OLIVE OIL

1 TEASPOON CHOPPED GARLIC

$1/4$ CUP PLUS 1 TABLESPOON FLOUR

2 TABLESPOONS TOMATO PURÉE

$1/2$ TEASPOON PLUS A PINCH OF FRESHLY GROUND NUTMEG

$1/8$ TEASPOON CINNAMON

$1/8$ TEASPOON OREGANO

$1/8$ TEASPOON THYME

1 CUP RED WINE

1 CUP CHICKEN STOCK

$1/2$ CUP GOLDEN RAISINS

SALT AND PEPPER

OIL FOR DEEP FRYING

3 ZUCCHINI

3 OUNCES FETA CHEESE, CRUMBLED

1 TABLESPOON BUTTER

2 TABLESPOONS DICED ONION

2 WHOLE CLOVES

2 BAY LEAVES

1 CUP MILK

WHITE PEPPER

1 BUNCH CHIVES, CHOPPED

1 TOMATO, PEELED, SEEDED, AND DICED

BONE AND SKIN THE DUCK, reserving the skin. Grind the meat and half of the skin (be sure to use the fatty skin from one of the breast pieces) using a medium sized plate in a meat grinder.

SAUTÉ THE EGGPLANT and shallots in the olive oil for 5 minutes, or until the shallots are tender. Add the garlic and cook for 1 minute. Add the duck meat and cook, stirring frequently, for 10 minutes, or until the duck is browned. Add $1/4$ cup of the flour and stir until combined. Add the tomato purée, $1/2$ teaspoon of the nutmeg, the cinnamon, oregano, and thyme and cook for 5 minutes, stirring constantly.

Stir in the wine and stock and simmer for 10 minutes. Remove from the heat and stir in the raisins. Season to taste with salt and pepper.

HEAT THE OIL to 350° in a deep fryer or heavy-bottomed pan. Trim the ends off the zucchini and, using a mandoline, cut lengthwise into $1/8$-inch-thick slices. Cook the zucchini in the oil for 10 seconds, or until tender. (If you do not have a deep fryer, sauté the slices with 1 tablespoon of oil for 1 minute, or until tender.) Remove the zucchini from the oil and drain on paper towels.

CUT THE REMAINING duck skin into $^1/_4$-inch pieces and place in a skillet over low heat for 5 minutes, or until some of the fat is rendered. Increase the heat to medium and cook for 10 minutes, or until crisp. Drain the cracklings on paper towels and season to taste with salt and pepper.

PREHEAT THE OVEN to 400°. Line six 4-ounce ramekins or soup cups with the zucchini, allowing the excess to hang over the sides of the cup. Fill the cups one-third of the way with the duck mixture, place $^1/_2$ ounce of the feta cheese in the center of each cup and top with the remaining duck. Fold the zucchini ends over to seal in the duck. Bake the moussaka for 5 to 7 minutes, or until hot.

MELT THE BUTTER in a small saucepan. Add the onion, whole cloves, and bay leaves and cook for 5 minutes, or until the onion is tender. Add the remaining 1 tablespoon of flour and pinch of nutmeg and cook for 3 to 4 minutes, or until bubbly. Whisk in the milk and simmer for 5 minutes. Strain through a fine-mesh sieve and season to taste with salt and white pepper.

UNMOLD A MOUSSAKA in the center of each plate. Spoon some of the sauce over each moussaka and sprinkle with the chives, cracklings, and tomato.

WINE SUGGESTION: Fruity red wine

Seared Duck Breasts
with Warm Lentil Salad

Garam masala is a blend of savory spices used in Indian cooking. It is a combination of coriander, black pepper, cardamom, cinnamon, caraway, cloves, ginger, and nutmeg. It can be found in specialty stores or online spice shops. Although it may take a little searching, garam masala gives the duck a great flavor that would be difficult to achieve otherwise.

Serves 8

- 1/4 CUP GARAM MASALA
- 2 TABLESPOONS SALT
- 2 TABLESPOONS BROWN SUGAR
- 8 DUCK BREASTS
- 1 MEDIUM ONION, FINELY DICED
- 1/2 CUP DICED CELERY
- 2 TABLESPOONS FINELY CHOPPED GARLIC
- 6 TABLESPOONS OLIVE OIL
- 2 TEASPOONS FINELY DICED ORANGE ZEST
- 3/4 CUP FRESHLY SQUEEZED ORANGE JUICE
- 6 CUPS CHICKEN STOCK
- 3 CUPS RED LENTILS
- 1 CUP CHOPPED GREEN ONIONS
- 2 ROMAINE HEARTS, QUARTERED
- 16 SMALL THISTLE FLOWERS, FOR GARNISH

COMBINE THE GARAM MASALA, salt, and 1 tablespoon of the brown sugar in a small bowl. Reserve 2 tablespoons of the mixture for the lentils. Spread the remaining spice mixture on both sides of the duck breasts, cover with plastic wrap, and refrigerate for 2 hours.

SAUTÉ THE ONION, celery, and garlic with the olive oil in a large saucepan for 5 to 7 minutes, or until tender. Add the zest, orange juice, chicken stock, lentils, and the reserved spice mixture and cook over medium-low heat for 40 minutes, or until the lentils are tender. Remove from the heat and stir in the green onions.

PREHEAT THE OVEN TO 350°. Place the duck breasts in an ovenproof sauté pan and cook, skin side down, over low heat for 10 minutes. Turn over the duck and sprinkle with the remaining 1 tablespoon of brown sugar. Bake for 5 minutes, remove the duck from the pan, and let rest for 5 minutes. Cut each breast in 1/4-inch-thick slices.

TOSS THE ROMAINE in the hot duck pan for 2 minutes, or until the edges just begin to wilt.

PLACE THE ROMAINE on one side of each plate and spoon the lentils alongside the lettuce. Fan the duck over the lentils and garnish with the thistle flowers.

🍇 WINE SUGGESTION: Medium-bodied red wine

CHILI-BRINED TURKEY WITH CHORIZO CORNBREAD STUFFING AND ORANGE-CHILI GLAZE

Marinating in brine makes this turkey extremely juicy and very flavorful. If you don't have a pot large enough to hold the turkey and the brine, you can use a cooler. Just place the turkey and brine in the cooler and add well-sealed bags of ice to keep it cool. This is a great preparation for a party because the brine, glaze, and cornbread are all prepared a day ahead. All you have to do on the day of the party is put together the stuffing and pop the bird in the oven.

SERVES 10

2½ GALLONS WATER

3⅓ CUPS SALT

3⅓ CUPS SUGAR

½ CUP MINCED GARLIC

½ CUP CHILI POWDER

1 TURKEY (15 TO 18 POUNDS)

CHORIZO CORNBREAD STUFFING (RECIPE FOLLOWS)

ORANGE-CHILI GLAZE, WARM (RECIPE FOLLOWS)

COMBINE THE WATER, salt, sugar, garlic, and chili powder in a large stockpot. Place the turkey in the pot, completely submerging it in the marinade. Refrigerate for 8 hours, or overnight.

PREHEAT THE OVEN to 425°. Remove the turkey from the marinade, rinse, and pat dry. Loosely fill the cavity of the turkey with the stuffing. Place the excess stuffing in a small roasting pan and bake during the last 45 minutes of the turkey's cooking time.

PLACE THE TURKEY in a roasting pan and cook for 30 minutes. Lower the oven temperature to 325° and cook for 2½ hours, or until the juices from the leg run clear. Baste the turkey with the Orange-Chili Glaze several times during the last 30 minutes of cooking. Remove the turkey from the oven and let rest for 20 minutes before slicing. Serve the remaining glaze in a small side dish.

🍇 WINE SUGGESTION: Crisp or semisweet white wine

Chorizo Cornbread Stuffing

MAKES ABOUT 3 QUARTS

CORNBREAD

1 CUP CORNMEAL

1 CUP FLOUR

2 TABLESPOONS SUGAR

1 TABLESPOON BAKING POWDER

1 TEASPOON SALT

$^1/_3$ CUP COLD BUTTER

2 EGGS

1 CUP MILK

8 CUPS CUBED DAY-OLD BREAD

1 POUND CHORIZO, CASING REMOVED

2 CELERY STALKS, DICED

2 MEDIUM ONIONS, DICED

2 JALAPEÑOS, DICED

1 CUP CHICKEN STOCK

1 TABLESPOON MEXICAN OREGANO LEAVES

$^1/_2$ CUP CHOPPED CILANTRO

SALT AND PEPPER

PREHEAT THE OVEN to 400°. Lightly grease a pie pan. Combine the cornmeal, flour, sugar, baking powder, and salt in a mixing bowl. Cut in the butter until well mixed. Stir in the eggs and milk. Pour the batter into the pie pan and cook for 25 minutes, or until light golden brown. (It is best to make the cornbread a day ahead and leave uncovered to dry slightly.)

CRUMBLE THE CORNBREAD in a large mixing bowl and add the bread cubes.

COOK THE CHORIZO for 7 to 10 minutes, or until browned. Add the celery, onions, and jalapeños and cook for 15 minutes, or until soft. Add the chorizo mixture, chicken stock, oregano, and cilantro to the cornbread mixture and stir until combined. Season to taste with salt and pepper.

Orange-Chili Glaze

MAKES APPROXIMATELY 1$^1/_4$ CUPS

8 OUNCES FROZEN ORANGE JUICE CONCENTRATE

2 TABLESPOONS CALIFORNIA CHILI POWDER

1 TEASPOON GROUND CUMIN

1 TEASPOON FINELY MINCED GARLIC

1$^1/_2$ TEASPOONS BLACK PEPPER

3 TABLESPOONS FRESHLY SQUEEZED LEMON JUICE

WHISK TOGETHER all of the ingredients, cover, and refrigerate for 24 hours.

Caribbean Jerk-Rubbed Pork Chops with Basmati Rice and Grilled Mango

Jerk spice originated in Jamaica, where it was a wet marinade. In America, we have changed it into a dry spice rub, but my version kind of splits the difference. The jerk rub adds many different layers of flavor to the pork chops, and when served with the mango, you can almost hear the steel drums.

Serves 4

2 TABLESPOONS ALLSPICE

1/4 TEASPOON NUTMEG

1 TEASPOON CINNAMON

2 TEASPOONS GROUND BLACK PEPPER

2 BUNCHES GREEN ONION, CHOPPED

6 JALAPEÑOS, SEEDED

1/3 CUP RED WINE VINEGAR

2 TABLESPOONS VEGETABLE OIL

2 TABLESPOONS SOY SAUCE

1 TABLESPOON SALT

8 PORK CHOPS

1 CUP BASMATI RICE

1 3/4 CUPS WATER

2 MANGOES, PEELED AND SLICED 1/4 INCH THICK

RUM BARBECUE SAUCE (RECIPE FOLLOWS)

4 MINT SPRIGS

PLACE THE ALLSPICE, nutmeg, cinnamon, pepper, green onions, jalapeños, vinegar, vegetable oil, soy sauce, and salt in a food processor and pulse until it forms a paste. Reserve 1 teaspoon and rub the remaining mixture on both sides of the pork chops. Cover and refrigerate for 8 hours, or overnight.

RINSE THE RICE under cold running water for 1 minute and drain. Place the rice, water, and the reserved spice rub in a saucepan and bring to a boil. Cover and simmer over medium-low heat for 15 to 20 minutes, or until the liquid is absorbed.

PREHEAT THE GRILL. Grill the mango slices for 1 minute on each side. Grill the pork chops for 5 to 7 minutes on each side, or until the desired doneness. Brush the pork chops with the Rum Barbecue Sauce for the last 2 minutes of cooking.

SPOON THE RICE on one side of each plate and top with a mint sprig. Arrange the mango slices next to the rice and place 2 of the pork chops alongside the mangoes and rice. Drizzle some of the sauce over the pork chops and around the plate.

Rum Barbecue Sauce
Makes approximately 1 1/4 cups

1 TABLESPOON BROWN SUGAR

1/2 CUP TOMATO SAUCE

1/4 CUP DARK RUM

1/4 CUP HONEY

1 TABLESPOON RED WINE VINEGAR

2 TABLESPOONS MINCED RED ONION

1 TABLESPOON MINCED GARLIC

3/4 TEASPOON WORCESTERSHIRE SAUCE

SALT AND PEPPER

WHISK TOGETHER all of the ingredients and refrigerate until ready to use.

🍇 WINE SUGGESTION: Fruity red wine

Pepper-Pecan Pork Tenderloin
with Potato Gratin

Pork really is the other white meat. In fact, pork tenderloin has less calories, less cholesterol, and only one more gram of fat than a skinless chicken breast. Because it is very lean, pork should not be over-cooked. Pork roasts should be cooked to slightly underdone and allowed to rest for 10 minutes to redistribute the juices. The result will be juicy meat with a slightly pink center.

Serves 8

3 LARGE POTATOES, PEELED AND THINLY SLICED

SALT AND PEPPER

1 EGG

2 CUPS WHIPPING CREAM

1 1/2 TEASPOONS CHOPPED GARLIC

1/2 CUP SHREDDED JACK CHEESE

1/2 CUP SHREDDED CHEDDAR CHEESE

1/2 CUP SHREDDED GRUYÈRE CHEESE

1/4 CUP CRACKED BLACK PEPPERCORNS

1 CUP FINELY CHOPPED PECANS

2 PORK TENDERLOINS, TRIMMED (1 TO 1 1/2 POUNDS EACH)

1 TABLESPOON EXTRA VIRGIN OLIVE OIL

1/4 CUP THINLY SLICED SHALLOTS

1/4 CUP PLUS 1 TEASPOON BUTTER, ROOM TEMPERATURE

1 CUP DRIED TART CHERRIES

1 CUP DRIED MISSION FIGS, QUARTERED

1 TABLESPOON BALSAMIC VINEGAR

1 TABLESPOON CABERNET SAUVIGNON

1 CUP DEMI-GLACE

PREHEAT THE OVEN TO 350°. Cook the potatoes in boiling salted water for 5 minutes, or until tender. Drain well, place in a 9-inch square baking pan, and season with salt and pepper. Combine the egg, cream, garlic, and 1/4 cup each of the Jack, Cheddar and Gruyère cheeses and pour over the potatoes. Combine the remaining 1/4 cup Jack, Cheddar, and Gruyère cheeses and sprinkle over the potatoes. Bake for 45 minutes, or until golden brown and bubbly. Let stand for 15 minutes before serving.

PREHEAT THE OVEN TO 400°. Combine the cracked pepper and pecans. Rub the tenderloins with the olive oil, season with salt, and coat with the cracked pepper mixture. Heat an ovenproof sauté pan over high heat and sear the tenderloins for 2 to 3 minutes on each side, or until browned. Place the pan in the oven and roast for 20 to 30 minutes, or until the internal temperature reaches 150°. Remove from the oven, let rest for 10 minutes, and slice.

SAUTÉ THE SHALLOTS in 1 teaspoon of the butter over medium heat for 5 minutes, or until tender. Add the cherries, figs, balsamic vinegar, wine, and demi-glace and simmer for 5 to 8 minutes, or until reduced to a saucelike consistency. Remove from the heat and gently stir in the remaining 1/4 cup of butter, 1 tablespoon at a time.

SPOON SOME OF THE SAUCE in the center of each plate and shingle the meat slices across the sauce. Place a scoop of the potato gratin alongside the meat and serve immediately.

🍇 WINE SUGGESTION: Full-bodied red wine

FRUIT-STUFFED PORK LOIN
WITH OBSESSION GLAZE

Here is the classic match of dried fruit and pork with a spiral effect that looks really impressive. I like to use the dark end of the pork loin for this dish because it's juicier and more tender. I used cherries, apricots, and raisins, but absolutely any combination of dried fruit works great.

SERVES 8 TO 10

- 2 CUPS IRONSTONE OBSESSION SYMPHONY
- 2 CUPS CHICKEN STOCK
- 3/4 CUP DRIED CHERRIES
- 3/4 CUP CHOPPED DRIED APRICOTS
- 1/4 CUP GOLDEN RAISINS
- 1/2 CUP CHOPPED SHALLOTS
- 1/2 CUP FRESH BREADCRUMBS
- 3/4 TEASPOON DRIED THYME
- 3/4 TEASPOON CHOPPED FRESH SAGE LEAVES
- 2 1/2 TO 3 POUNDS PORK LOIN
- SALT AND PEPPER
- 2 TABLESPOONS EXTRA VIRGIN OLIVE OIL
- 1/4 CUP APRICOT JAM
- 1 TABLESPOON CORNSTARCH
- 3 TABLESPOONS BUTTER, AT ROOM TEMPERATURE

BRING THE WINE and chicken stock to a boil. Add the dried cherries, apricots, and raisins, remove from the heat, and let stand for 20 minutes. Strain through a fine-mesh sieve, reserving the liquid and fruit separately.

COMBINE THE DRIED FRUIT, shallots, bread-crumbs, thyme, and sage in a bowl. Cut the pork loin lengthwise, two-thirds of the way through and spread it open like a book. Cut each of the halves two-thirds of the way through from the center toward the outer edge. Lay the pork flat and cover with plastic wrap. Pound the meat to a fairly even 1/4- to 1/2-inch thickness. Season the meat with salt and pepper and spread the fruit mixture over the pork. Tightly roll up the pork and tie with kitchen string.

PREHEAT THE OVEN to 400°. Heat the olive oil in an ovenproof sauté pan. Season the outside of the pork with salt and pepper and sear for 2 to 3 minutes on each side, or until browned. Place the pan in the oven and roast, basting occasionally with 3/4 cup of the liquid from the fruit, for 30 to 40 minutes, or until slightly less than the desired doneness. Let rest for 10 minutes and cut into 1/2-inch-thick slices.

WHILE THE PORK is cooking, place the remaining liquid from the fruit in a small saucepan and cook for 30 minutes, or until reduced to about 1 1/4 cups. Add the apricot jam and cook until smooth. Mix the cornstarch with a little of the fruit liquid to create a slurry. Stir the slurry into the sauce, bring to a boil, and remove from the heat. Stir in the butter, 1 tablespoon at a time, just prior to serving.

SHINGLE THE PORK SLICES down the center of a serving platter and spoon the sauce over the pork and around the plate. Serve any extra sauce on the side.

WINE SUGGESTION: Semisweet white wine

FENNEL-CRUSTED PORK LOIN
WITH BRAISED CABBAGE

I actually adapted this recipe from a casserole my wife, Monica, made using leftover pork and cabbage. I loved the classic pairing of pork, fennel, and cabbage with the added richness of the cream and cheese. I like to serve this with horseradish mashed potatoes to add a little bite and help cut the richness.

SERVES 8

½ CUP PLUS 1 TABLESPOON FENNEL SEED

¼ CUP CHOPPED GARLIC

¼ CUP EXTRA VIRGIN OLIVE OIL

1 TABLESPOON SALT

1 TABLESPOON PEPPER

4 POUNDS BONELESS PORK CENTER LOIN

⅔ CUP FINELY CHOPPED ONION

¼ CUP BUTTER

1 LARGE HEAD GREEN CABBAGE, SHREDDED

1⅓ CUPS WHIPPING CREAM

1½ TEASPOONS PAPRIKA

1½ CUPS GRATED GRUYÈRE CHEESE

FENNEL FRONDS, FOR GARNISH

PREHEAT THE OVEN to 375°. In a blender or spice grinder, grind ½ cup of the fennel seeds to a coarse powder. Add the garlic, olive oil, salt, and pepper and blend until it forms a paste. Rub the paste evenly over the pork loin and roast for 30 to 40 minutes, or until the internal temperature reaches 150°. Remove from the oven and let rest for 10 minutes.

WHILE THE PORK IS COOKING, sauté the onions and the remaining 1 tablespoon of fennel seeds in the butter for 10 minutes, or until the onions are tender. Add the cabbage and cook over high heat for 3 minutes, stirring frequently to avoid browning. Add the cream and paprika and bring to a boil. Reduce to medium heat and cook for 8 to 10 minutes, or until reduced to a saucelike consistency.

PLACE THE CABBAGE on an ovenproof platter and top with the Gruyère cheese. Bake for 5 minutes, or until the cheese is melted.

THINLY SLICE THE PORK LOIN, place in the center of the cabbage, and garnish with the fennel fronds.

 WINE SUGGESTION: Barrel-fermented or light and fruity white wine

Peanut-Crusted Lamb Rack with Merlot Mashed Potatoes and Apple Cider Demi-Glace

Here is another guaranteed-to-impress dish that is not difficult to prepare. There are only two things you need to know: Watch the shallots carefully toward the end of cooking, there is a very fine line between the liquid being evaporated and the shallots being hopelessly burned. And, barely fold the shallots into the potatoes. They will still taste great if you overmix, but the potatoes will turn an unappetizing reddish purple color.

Serves 4

- 2^1/$_2$ CUPS PLUS 2 TABLESPOONS APPLE CIDER
- 1 TEASPOON MINCED GARLIC
- 1 TEASPOON MINCED GINGER
- 1 CUP DEMI-GLACE
- ^{1}/$_2$ CUP MERLOT
- ^{1}/$_4$ CUP BUTTER, AT ROOM TEMPERATURE
- 1 CUP UNSALTED ROASTED PEANUTS

- ^{1}/$_2$ CUP BREADCRUMBS
- 2 EGGS
- 2 LAMB RACKS (OR 8 LAMB CHOPS)
- SALT AND PEPPER
- FLOUR FOR DUSTING
- ^{1}/$_4$ CUP VEGETABLE OIL
- MERLOT MASHED POTATOES (RECIPE FOLLOWS)

PLACE 2^1/$_2$ CUPS of the apple cider, the garlic, and ginger in a small saucepan and simmer over medium heat for 30 minutes, or until reduced to about ^{3}/$_4$ cup. Add the demi-glace and the wine and cook for 30 minutes, or until reduced to about 1^1/$_4$ cups. Remove the pan from the heat and set aside. Just prior to serving, reheat the sauce and whisk in the butter, 2 tablespoons at a time.

PULSE THE PEANUTS and breadcrumbs in a food processor until they reach a coarse breadcrumb consistency. (The breadcrumbs will keep the peanuts from turning to butter.)

PREHEAT THE OVEN to 400°. Whisk together the eggs and the remaining 2 tablespoons of apple cider in a large bowl. Season the lamb racks with salt and pepper and lightly dust with the flour. Dip the meaty side of the racks in the egg mixture and coat with the peanuts. Heat the oil in a large ovenproof sauté pan over high heat and sear the racks for 2 to 3 minutes on all sides. Place racks, peanut side up, in the pan and roast in the oven for 20 minutes, or until slightly less than the desired doneness. Let rest for 10 minutes and cut each rack into 4 chops.

PLACE A SCOOP of the Merlot Mashed Potatoes on one side of each plate. Spoon some of the sauce next to the potatoes and lean 2 lamb chops against the potatoes.

continued

Merlot Mashed Potatoes

SERVES 4

¹/₄ CUP COARSELY DICED SHALLOT

¹/₄ CUP PLUS 1 TEASPOON UNSALTED BUTTER

1 CUP MERLOT

2 POUNDS POTATOES, PEELED AND ROUGHLY CHOPPED

¹/₄ CUP WHIPPING CREAM

SALT AND WHITE PEPPER

COOK THE SHALLOT in 1 teaspoon of the butter over low heat for 5 minutes, or until translucent. Add the wine and cook over medium heat for 30 minutes, or until all of the liquid has evaporated. Watch carefully toward the end of the cooking process so the shallots don't burn.

COOK THE POTATOES in boiling salted water for 20 minutes, or until tender. Drain the potatoes and add the cream and the remaining ¹/₄ cup of butter to the pan. Bring to a boil and remove from the heat. Place the potatoes back in the pan and, using a hand masher, mash the potatoes until the cream and butter are incorporated, but the mixture is still chunky. Season to taste with salt and white pepper. Gently fold in the shallots just prior to serving.

🍇 WINE SUGGESTION: Light or medium-bodied red wine

LAMB WELLINGTON

Here is a little twist on a traditional Wellington. The lamb loins are cooked whole and sliced so when it's plated you see the beautiful layers of pastry, mushrooms, and lamb. I think the sauce is a perfect match for this dish. The red wine really accents the earthy mushrooms and the hint of mint is enough to satisfy any traditionalist.

SERVES 6

2 TABLESPOONS OLIVE OIL

2 LAMB RACKS, BONED, TRIMMINGS RESERVED

SALT AND PEPPER

3 CUPS MINCED CREMINI MUSHROOMS

1/4 CUP MINCED SHALLOT

1 1/2 TABLESPOONS MINCED GARLIC

1/2 TEASPOON DRIED BASIL

1/2 TEASPOON DRIED ROSEMARY

1/2 TEASPOON DRIED THYME

1/2 TEASPOON DRIED OREGANO

1 1/2 TEASPOONS PEPPER

1 1/2 CUPS RED WINE

2 PUFF PASTRY SHEETS

1 EGG, BEATEN

1/2 CUP SUGAR

1/4 CUP RED WINE VINEGAR

1/2 TEASPOON MINCED GARLIC

1 TABLESPOON CHOPPED FRESH MINT

2 TABLESPOONS BUTTER, AT ROOM TEMPERATURE

PLACE THE OLIVE OIL in a large sauté pan over high heat. Season the lamb loins with salt and pepper and sear the lamb on all sides. Remove the lamb from the pan and set aside.

MINCE THE RESERVED LAMB trimmings and cook for 2 to 3 minutes, or until browned. Add the mushrooms, shallot, garlic, basil, rosemary, thyme, oregano, and pepper and cook for 1 minute. Add 1 cup of the wine and bring to a boil. Reduce the heat to medium and simmer for 20 minutes, or until dry. Remove from the heat and let cool to room temperature.

PREHEAT THE OVEN to 400°. Lay out the puff pastry sheets and spread the mushroom mixture over the sheets. Place a lamb loin on each pastry sheet and roll the pastry around the lamb. Place the Wellingtons on a parchment-lined baking sheet,

seam side down, tucking the ends of the dough underneath to completely seal the lamb. Brush with the egg and bake for 20 to 25 minutes, or until golden brown. Remove from the oven, let rest for 5 minutes, and cut each Wellington into 9 slices.

MEANWHILE, BRING THE SUGAR, the remaining 1/2 cup of wine, and the vinegar to a boil in a small saucepan. Simmer for 30 to 40 minutes, or until reduced to a scant 1/2 cup. Stir in the garlic and mint and remove from the heat. Add the butter and stir until incorporated.

PLACE 3 SLICES of the Wellington in the center of each plate and drizzle with the sauce.

🍇 WINE SUGGESTION: Fruity red wine

SIZZLIN' HOT RIB-EYE STEAK WITH SHAFT BLUE CHEESE BUTTER

This is one of the most flavorful marinades I have ever made and it's so easy it's almost embarrassing. This steak can be quite spicy, but the blue cheese butter helps to put out the fire. I use Shaft blue cheese, which is literally aged in an old gold mine shaft, but any good blue cheese will work well.

SERVES 4

- 1/2 CUP TABASCO SAUCE
- 1/4 CUP WORCESTERSHIRE SAUCE
- 2 TABLESPOONS MINCED GARLIC
- 1/4 CUP PLUS 2 TABLESPOONS EXTRA VIRGIN OLIVE OIL
- 1 TEASPOON FRESHLY GROUND BLACK PEPPER
- 4 BONE-IN RIB-EYE STEAKS (1 TO 1 1/2 POUNDS EACH)

- 4 SLICES FRENCH BREAD
- 2 TABLESPOONS MELTED BUTTER
- 4 SMALL TOMATOES, HALVED
- 1 POUND ASPARAGUS SPEARS, TRIMMED
- KOSHER SALT AND PEPPER
- SHAFT BLUE CHEESE BUTTER (RECIPE FOLLOWS)

COMBINE THE TABASCO SAUCE, Worcestershire sauce, garlic, 1/4 cup of the olive oil, and black pepper in a small bowl. Coat both sides of each steak with the marinade, cover, and refrigerate for at least 2 hours, or overnight.

PREHEAT THE OVEN TO 375°. Place the bread slices on a baking sheet and brush with the melted butter. Bake for 5 to 7 minutes, or until golden brown.

PREHEAT THE GRILL. Brush the tomato halves and asparagus spears with the remaining 2 tablespoons of olive oil. Place the tomatoes on the grill, cut side up, and cook for 5 to 7 minutes, or until soft. Grill the asparagus, turning occasionally, for 5 to 7 minutes, or until tender. Season the steaks with salt and pepper and grill for 5 to 8 minutes on each side, or until cooked to the desired doneness.

PLACE A TOASTED BREAD SLICE on one edge of the plate and top with a steak. Arrange the asparagus and tomato halves around the plate and top the steak with a large dollop of the Shaft Blue Cheese Butter.

🍇 WINE SUGGESTION: Medium-bodied or fruity red wine

Shaft Blue Cheese Butter

MAKES ABOUT 1 CUP

1/4 CUP GARLIC CLOVES

2 TABLESPOONS EXTRA VIRGIN OLIVE OIL

1/2 CUP BUTTER

1/4 CUP CRUMBLED SHAFT BLUE CHEESE

1 1/2 TEASPOONS CHOPPED FRESH OREGANO

1/2 TEASPOON COARSELY GROUND BLACK PEPPER

SALT

PREHEAT THE OVEN to 325°. Toss the garlic cloves in the oil in a small baking pan and cover tightly with aluminum foil. Roast for 10 to 15 minutes, or until tender. Cool completely and squeeze the roasted garlic from the cloves.

COMBINE THE ROASTED GARLIC, butter, blue cheese, oregano, and black pepper in a small bowl and season to taste with salt. Refrigerate until ready to use.

CABERNET-MARINATED TRI-TIP ROAST
WITH GRILLED VEGETABLES

Tri-tip is a cut of meat that has been used in restaurants for years, but only recently started appearing in supermarkets. It is part of the bottom sirloin and, in its former life, was sold as part of a sirloin roast. It is a very flavorful cut of meat that is best if marinated and not overcooked.

SERVES 6

2 1/2 CUPS CABERNET SAUVIGNON

8 GARLIC CLOVES, CRUSHED

2 TABLESPOONS BLACK PEPPER

2 TABLESPOONS SOY SAUCE

2 TABLESPOONS RED WINE VINEGAR

1 ONION, CHOPPED

2 CUPS CANOLA OIL

3 TABLESPOONS SALT

5 BAY LEAVES

1/4 CUP FRESH ROSEMARY LEAVES

PINCH OF DRIED OREGANO

PINCH OF DRIED BASIL

3 TO 3 1/2 POUNDS TRI-TIP ROAST

SALT AND PEPPER

1/4 CUP EXTRA VIRGIN OLIVE OIL

2 TABLESPOONS BALSAMIC VINEGAR

1 SMALL FENNEL BULB, CUT IN
   1/4-INCH-THICK SLICES

1 SMALL SUMMER SQUASH, CUT IN
   1/4-INCH-THICK SLICES

1 RED ONION, CUT IN 1/4-INCH-THICK SLICES

1 RED BELL PEPPER, SEEDED AND HALVED

COMBINE THE WINE, garlic, pepper, soy sauce, red wine vinegar, onion, oil, salt, bay leaves, rosemary, oregano, and basil in a large bowl. Place the roast in the bowl and completely submerge the meat in the marinade. Refrigerate for 3 to 5 days. (The meat must be completely submerged in the marinade to prevent bacteria growth.)

PREHEAT THE GRILL. Remove the tri-tip from the marinade, pat dry, and season with salt and pepper. Grill for 10 to 15 minutes on each side, or until cooked medium-rare. Let rest for 10 minutes and cut into 1/4-inch-thick slices.

COMBINE THE OLIVE OIL and balsamic vinegar in a small bowl. Brush the fennel, squash, onion, and red bell pepper with the olive oil mixture and grill for 4 to 5 minutes on each side, or until tender. Remove the vegetables from the grill, cut into bite-sized pieces, and toss together.

SPOON SOME OF THE VEGETABLES on one side of each plate and shingle the beef slices alongside the vegetables.

🍇 WINE SUGGESTION: Medium-bodied red wine

CHILI-CITRUS STEAK WITH CHILI-ROASTED POTATOES

Forget everything you have heard, you can serve white wine with steak. Because of the fresh, green flavors of the marinade, this steak actually pairs best with Chardonnay. Everyone thinks I'm crazy when they see this pairing, but try it and you'll see it's a great match.

SERVES 4

- ¼ CUP CUMIN SEEDS, TOASTED
- ⅓ CUP CHOPPED GARLIC
- 8 JALAPEÑO PEPPERS, SEEDED
- 1 TEASPOON SALT
- 1 CUP EXTRA VIRGIN OLIVE OIL
- ½ CUP FRESHLY SQUEEZED LIME JUICE
- ½ CUP FRESHLY SQUEEZED ORANGE JUICE
- 1 TABLESPOON SHERRY VINEGAR
- 1 TABLESPOON BLACK PEPPER
- 2½ POUNDS BEEF TENDERLOIN

- 1 POUND SMALL RED POTATOES, HALVED
- ½ TEASPOON GARLIC POWDER
- 1 TEASPOON CHILI POWDER
- 2 RED ONIONS, SLICED
- SALT AND PEPPER
- 8 FLOUR TORTILLAS
- 1 AVOCADO, PEELED AND SLICED
- ASSORTED SMALL PEPPERS, FOR GARNISH
- 4 LIME WEDGES
- 4 CILANTRO SPRIGS

CRUSH THE CUMIN SEEDS and place in a blender with the garlic, jalapeño, salt, ¾ cup of the olive oil, the lime juice, orange juice, vinegar, and pepper. Blend on high speed for 10 seconds, or until finely chopped.

SLICE THE MEAT lengthwise into ¾-inch-thick slabs. Place the meat in a nonreactive pan and pour half of the marinade over the meat. Cover and refrigerate for 1 to 3 hours.

PREHEAT THE OVEN to 400°. Place the potatoes on a baking sheet and toss with 2 tablespoons of the olive oil, the garlic powder, and chili powder. Roast the potatoes for 20 to 30 minutes, or until tender.

PREHEAT THE GRILL. Brush the onions with the remaining 2 tablespoons of olive oil and season with salt and pepper. Grill the onions and beef for 3 to 4 minutes on each side, or until the beef is cooked rare. Let rest for 5 minutes and slice the meat in ¼-inch-thick strips.

PLACE SOME OF THE POTATOES on one side of each plate. Fan the beef slices next to the potatoes and top with the grilled onions. Spoon the reserved marinade over the meat and onions. Fold the tortillas and place the on the edge of the plate. Arrange the avocado, peppers, and lime wedges around the plate and top with a cilantro sprig.

WINE SUGGESTION: Crisp white wine

PEPPERED BEEF TENDERLOIN with WILD RICE and DRIED FRUIT–BRANDY SAUCE

Demi-glace is becoming more readily available at supermarkets, but you can also make your own. Make a basic veal stock, strain it, and cook it over low heat for several hours. One gallon of stock should be reduced down to about 2 cups of demi-glace. Freeze any extra in ice cube trays so you can easily take out just the amount that you need.

SERVES 8

- 2 TABLESPOONS DRIED BLUEBERRIES
- 2 TABLESPOONS DRIED CHERRIES
- 2 TABLESPOONS DRIED CRANBERRIES
- 1/2 CUP DRIED STRAWBERRIES
- 1/2 CUP BRANDY
- 1/4 CUP DICED ONION
- 1 TABLESPOON BUTTER
- 2 CUPS WILD RICE
- 8 CUPS CHICKEN STOCK

- 1 ORANGE, HALVED
- 1 TEASPOON MINCED SHALLOTS
- 1 TEASPOON EXTRA VIRGIN OLIVE OIL
- 1/2 CUP MERLOT
- 1/2 CUP DEMI-GLACE
- 1/4 CUP BUTTER, AT ROOM TEMPERATURE
- 3 POUNDS BEEF TENDERLOIN, TRIMMED
- SALT
- 1 TABLESPOON CRACKED PEPPERCORNS

SOAK THE BLUEBERRIES, cherries, cranberries, and strawberries in the brandy overnight.

SAUTÉ THE ONION in the 1 tablespoon of butter for 5 minutes, or until tender. Add the wild rice and chicken stock to the pan. Squeeze the juice from the orange into the pan and add the orange halves. Bring to a boil, cover, and simmer for 45 to 60 minutes, or until the rice is tender. Remove the orange halves from the pan and fluff the rice with a fork.

SAUTÉ THE SHALLOT in 1/2 teaspoon of the olive oil for 1 minute in a small saucepan. Add the dried fruit and brandy mixture and bring to a boil. Simmer for 5 minutes, or until the liquid is reduced to about 1/4 cup. Add 1/4 cup of the wine and cook for 4 minutes, or until reduced to about 1/4 cup. Add the demi-glace and simmer for 10 minutes. Just prior to serving, add the remaining 1/4 cup wine and stir in the room temperature butter.

PREHEAT THE OVEN to 400°. Season the beef with salt and sprinkle with the cracked peppercorns. Heat the remaining 1/2 teaspoon of olive oil in a oven-proof skillet over high heat. Sear the tenderloin for 2 to 3 minutes on each side, or until browned. Place the skillet in the oven and roast for 20 minutes, or until slightly less than the desired doneness. Allow the tenderloin to rest for 10 minutes and cut into 1/2-inch-thick slices.

PLACE SOME OF THE WILD RICE on one side of each plate. Spoon the sauce next to the rice and fan the tenderloin slices over the sauce.

🍇 WINE SUGGESTION: Light bodied red wine

MUSHROOM AND ROQUEFORT–STUFFED VENISON WITH PORT DEMI-GLACE

This extremely elegant dish is much simpler to prepare than it looks. The only challenge here is understanding how to cut open the roast. Think of the roast as a jelly roll you are trying to unroll. Every time you make a cut you have to push the jelly roll open in order to make the next cut. Don't worry if it's a little uneven when you are cutting, pounding will even it out a lot. And, as you can see by the photo, it doesn't need to be perfect.

SERVES 4

1 CUP SLICED SHIITAKE MUSHROOMS

1 CUP SLICED CREMINI MUSHROOMS

1 CUP SLICED CHANTERELLE MUSHROOMS

1/4 CUP PLUS 2 TABLESPOONS BUTTER

2 TABLESPOONS FINELY DICED SHALLOT

1 TEASPOON MINCED GARLIC

1/4 CUP CRUMBLED ROQUEFORT CHEESE

1 CUP PORT

1 CUP DEMI-GLACE

1 1/2 POUNDS VENISON LOIN ROAST

SALT AND PEPPER

1 TABLESPOON EXTRA VIRGIN OLIVE OIL

2 POUNDS YUKON GOLD POTATOES, PEELED AND ROUGHLY CHOPPED

1/4 CUP WHIPPING CREAM

WHITE PEPPER

1 TABLESPOON CHOPPED CHIVES

24 GREEN BEANS, STEAMED

8 LONG-CUT CHIVES

SAUTÉ THE SHIITAKE, cremini, and chanterelle mushrooms in 2 tablespoons of the butter over medium heat for 15 minutes, or until the mushrooms are browned. Remove from the heat, add the shallot and garlic, and stir until thoroughly combined. Place the mixture in a bowl, add the Roquefort, and toss quickly to evenly distribute the cheese.

POUR THE PORT into the pan from the mushrooms and cook over medium heat for 10 minutes, or until reduced to about 3/4 cup. Add the demi-glace and cook for 15 minutes, or until reduced to about 1 cup. Reheat just prior to serving.

MAKE A LENGTHWISE CUT in the venison roast about 1/2 inch from one side, going down to about 1/2 inch from the bottom of the roast. Open the roast like a book, lay your knife blade on the thin side, and slice to about 1/2 inch from the opposite edge of the roast. Continue opening and slicing the roast until it is completely "unrolled". Cover the venison with plastic wrap and pound with a meat mallet until fairly even in thickness.

PREHEAT THE OVEN to 400°. Season the venison with salt and pepper. Evenly spread the mushroom mixture over the meat, leaving a 2-inch edge on one end. Carefully roll up the roast and tie closed with kitchen string. Heat the olive oil over medium-high heat. Sear the venison roll for 2 minutes on each

side, or until completely browned. Place the venison in an ovenproof pan and roast for 10 to 15 minutes, or until the internal temperature reaches 120°. Remove the venison from the oven and let rest for 10 minutes. Cut into 8 slices just prior to serving.

MEANWHILE, COOK THE POTATOES in boiling salted water for 20 minutes, or until tender. Drain the potatoes and add the cream and the remaining $1/4$ cup of butter to the pan. Bring to a boil and remove from the heat. Using a hand mixer, mash the potatoes until creamy. Season to taste with salt and white pepper and fold in the chopped chives.

PLACE SOME OF THE MASHED POTATOES slightly off center on each plate. Arrange the green beans alongside the potatoes and lean 2 venison slices against the potatoes. Drizzle the sauce around the plate and garnish with the long-cut chives.

🍇 WINE SUGGESTION: Full-bodied red wine

DESSERTS

SUMMER FRUIT TART

I have made at least twenty different versions of this tart: pear and ginger, raspberry and blackberry, and even caramelized apple. But, no matter what combination you choose, it is always quick, easy, and delicious. This tart is also wonderful with the Obsession Sauce on page 134 or vanilla ice cream.

SERVES 8

- 1 PUFF PASTRY SHEET
- 3 PEACHES, PEELED AND HALVED
- 3 PLUMS, SLICED $1/4$ INCH THICK
- $1/2$ CUP BLACKBERRIES
- $1/4$ CUP SUGAR
- 1 TABLESPOON BUTTER

PLACE THE PUFF PASTRY on a baking sheet. Toss together the peaches, plums, blackberries, and sugar in a mixing bowl and spoon into the center of the puff pastry. Fold up the edges of the pastry to create a free-form tart. Refrigerate for 30 minutes before baking.

PREHEAT THE OVEN to 400°. Dot the butter over the fruit and bake the tart for 25 minutes, or until golden brown.

SLICE THE TART into 8 pieces, reserving any juice that is released. Spoon the reserved juice over the slices just prior to serving.

WINE SUGGESTION: Semisweet white wine

APPLE-BRANDY TART

This rustic tart is one of my children's favorite desserts. The puff pastry forms a wonderful crispy crust that adds a great texture. Served with a scoop of vanilla ice cream melting on top, this is sure to be a crowd- pleaser.

SERVES 8

1/2 CUP BUTTER

3/4 CUP BROWN SUGAR

7 APPLES, PEELED, CORED, AND HALVED

2 TABLESPOONS APPLE BRANDY OR BRANDY

PINCH OF SALT

CINNAMON

1 PUFF PASTRY SHEET

PLACE THE BUTTER and sugar in a 9-inch oven-proof sauté pan and arrange the apple halves in the pan. Sauté the apples over medium-high heat, turning occasionally, for 15 minutes, or until the sugar is caramelized and the apples are brown. Add the apple brandy, salt, and cinnamon to taste and turn the apples in the pan until the brandy is incorporated. Remove from the heat and set aside.

PREHEAT THE OVEN to 400°. Cut a 9-inch circle from the puff pastry. Cut the trimmed dough into 1/2-inch-wide strips and piece together a rim around the edge of the pastry. Place the pastry circle, rim side down, on top of the cooked apples and bake for 10 to 15 minutes, or until golden brown. Remove the pan from oven and turn over onto a serving plate. Cool slightly and cut into 8 pieces. Serve warm.

BEVERAGE SUGGESTION: Brandy

Raspberry-Stuffed Poached Peaches with Obsession Sauce

The hardest part of this dish is getting the pits out of the peaches without mangling them. The easiest way that I have found is to cut the top off of the peaches, exposing the top of the pit, and then wiggling the pits back and forth until they loosen enough to pull them out.

Serves 6

6 FREESTONE PEACHES

4 CUPS IRONSTONE OBSESSION SYMPHONY

1/2 CUP SUGAR

1 CUP CRUSHED RASPBERRIES

OBSESSION SAUCE (RECIPE FOLLOWS)

6 MINT SPRIGS

CAREFULLY REMOVE THE PITS from the peaches, leaving the peaches whole. Bring the wine and 1/4 cup of the sugar to a boil and add the peaches. Cook for 10 minutes, or until the peaches are tender. Drain the peaches, remove their skins, and refrigerate until chilled.

COMBINE THE RASPBERRIES and the remaining 1/4 cup of sugar and let stand until the sugar dissolves.

PLACE A PEACH in the center of each plate and spoon some of the raspberries inside each peach. Spoon the Obsession Sauce over the peach and around the plates and garnish with the mint sprigs.

Obsession Sauce
MAKES APPROXIMATELY 2 CUPS

6 EGG YOLKS

1/4 CUP SUGAR

1/4 CUP IRONSTONE OBSESSION SYMPHONY

PINCH OF SALT

WHISK TOGETHER all the ingredients in the top of a double boiler. Cook over barely simmering water, whisking constantly, for 10 minutes, or until it reaches the consistency of thin cream soup. Remove from the heat and whip on high speed for 3 to 5 minutes, or until thick and the volume has doubled. Serve immediately.

🍇 WINE SUGGESTION: Semisweet white wine

Raspberry Purses

Mascarpone is an Italian cheese that is creamier and slightly sweeter than cream cheese. If you can't find it at your local market, you can combine 4 ounces of softened cream cheese, 1½ tablespoons of sour cream, 2 tablespoons of whipping cream, and 1 teaspoon of confectioners' sugar as a good substitute.

Serves 6

⅔ CUP MASCARPONE CHEESE

3 TABLESPOONS CONFECTIONERS' SUGAR

2 TABLESPOONS IRONSTONE OBSESSION SYMPHONY

9 FILO DOUGH SHEETS

¼ CUP BUTTER, MELTED

2½ TO 3 CUPS RASPBERRIES

1 CUP WHIPPING CREAM

6 MINT SPRIGS

COMBINE THE MASCARPONE, 1 tablespoon of the confectioners' sugar, and 1 tablespoon of the wine in a small bowl.

PREHEAT THE OVEN to 375°. Lay out 1 sheet of the filo on a work surface and lightly brush with the butter. Cover with a second sheet of filo, brush with butter, and top with a third sheet of filo. Cut the filo stack into 4 long strips. Place a small spoonful of the mascarpone mixture and 3 or 4 raspberries at one end of each strip and fold in a triangular flag fold. Brush the outside of each triangle liberally with butter, sealing any loose ends, and place on a parchment-lined baking sheet. Repeat the process with the remaining filo sheets and filling. Bake for 10 to 12 minutes, or until golden brown.

LIGHTLY WHIP THE CREAM and the remaining 2 tablespoons of confectioners' sugar until it reaches a thick, saucelike consistency (not until it becomes whipped cream). Stir in the remaining 1 tablespoon of wine.

SPOON THE CREAM into the center of each plate. Arrange 2 of the raspberry purses on the cream and garnish with the remaining berries and mint sprigs.

BEVERAGE SUGGESTION: Grand Marnier

APRICOT SYMPHONY TRIANGLES

Working with filo dough can be a bit of a challenge, but it is made easier by following these tips: Always thaw filo in the refrigerator; thawing it at room temperature promotes condensation, which causes the layers to stick together. Always keep filo dough covered with a slightly damp paper towel while working with it to keep it from drying out. Once you get the hang of working with filo dough these will go very quickly.

SERVES 8

- 3/4 CUP IRONSTONE OBSESSION SYMPHONY
- 3/4 CUP SUGAR
- 6 OUNCES DRIED APRICOTS, CHOPPED
- 1/3 CUP SLICED GINGER
- 2 TABLESPOONS FRESHLY SQUEEZED LEMON JUICE

- 5 1/2 TABLESPOONS BUTTER
- 12 FILO DOUGH SHEETS
- 5 AMARETTI COOKIES, CRUSHED
- 2 1/2 OUNCES WHITE CHOCOLATE, SLICED

BRING THE WINE, sugar, apricots, ginger, and lemon juice to a boil in a small saucepan. Simmer over low heat for 45 minutes, or until the liquid is reduced to about 3/4 cup. Strain the sauce through a fine-mesh sieve, saving the liquid and apricots separately and discarding the ginger.

MELT 1/4 CUP OF THE BUTTER. Lay out 1 sheet of the filo on a work surface, lightly brush with the melted butter, and sprinkle with some of the crushed cookies. Top with a second filo sheet, brush with melted butter, and sprinkle with the cookies. Top with a third filo sheet and brush with melted butter. Cut the filo stack into 6 equal strips.

PREHEAT THE OVEN to 375°. Set aside 2 tablespoons each of the apricots and the white chocolate for garnish. Place some of the remaining apricots and chocolate evenly in the lower left corner of each filo strip. Fold the strips in a triangular flag fold, getting the corners as tight as possible to prevent the chocolate from leaking out during cooking. Brush the triangles liberally with the

melted butter, sealing any loose ends, and place on a parchment-lined baking sheet. Repeat the process with the remaining filo sheets and filling. Bake for 10 to 12 minutes, or until golden brown.

WARM THE SAUCE and stir in the remaining 1 1/2 tablespoons of butter until completely incorporated.

PLACE 3 TRIANGLES in the center of each plate and drizzle with the sauce. Sprinkle the remaining apricots and white chocolate around the plates.

🍇 WINE SUGGESTION: Semisweet white wine

BLUEBERRY NAPOLEON

The lesson you should learn from this recipe is simple: If you have puff pastry in your freezer you can always come up with a quick, delicious, impressive dessert. This Napoleon can be made with fresh or frozen fruit, the whipped cream can be flavored with extracts or liqueurs, or you can use softened cream cheese instead of the whipped cream. The possibilities are endless.

SERVES 6

1/4 CUP CONFECTIONERS' SUGAR

1 CUP COLD WATER

3 CUPS BLUEBERRIES

6 3-INCH PUFF PASTRY CIRCLES

1 CUP WHIPPING CREAM

6 MINT SPRIGS

COMBINE 2 TABLESPOONS of the confectioners' sugar and the water in a small saucepan. Add 1 cup of the blueberries and bring to a boil. Simmer for 5 minutes, smashing the blueberries with a fork during cooking. Strain through a fine-mesh sieve, discarding the solids, and refrigerate for 1 hour, or until chilled.

PREHEAT THE OVEN to 400°. Place the puff pastry on a parchment-lined baking sheet and bake for 15 minutes, or until golden brown. Cool and slice each pastry in half horizontally, leaving two thin circles.

WHIP THE CREAM with the remaining 2 tablespoons of confectioners' sugar until soft peaks form. Gently fold in 1 1/2 cups of blueberries, being careful not to smash them.

SPREAD SOME OF THE BLUEBERRY sauce in the center of each plate and place the bottom half of the puff pastry on the sauce. Spoon some of the berry cream onto the pastry and cover with the puff pastry top. Spoon more of the berry cream on top of the pastry and drizzle the berry sauce over the cream and around the plate. Sprinkle the remaining 1/2 cup of blueberries around the plates and garnish with the mint sprigs.

BEVERAGE SUGGESTION: Lighter-style port

Grilled Mango Sundae
with Myers's Rum Sauce

This is a perfect dessert to serve after the Caribbean Jerk-Rubbed Pork Chops (page 164). The mango can be grilled when you are cooking the pork chops and warmed in the sauce just prior to serving.

Serves 4

2 MANGOES, PEELED AND SLICED $1/4$ INCH THICK

$3/4$ CUP BROWN SUGAR

$3/4$ CUP MYERS'S RUM

3 TABLESPOONS BUTTER

1 PINT VANILLA ICE CREAM

4 MINT SPRIGS

PREHEAT THE GRILL. Toss the mango slices with $1/4$ cup of the brown sugar and $1/4$ cup of the rum. Grill the mango slices for 2 minutes on each side. Let cool and cut each slice into thirds.

PLACE THE REMAINING $1/2$ cup sugar, $1/2$ cup rum, and the butter in a small saucepan over medium heat. Bring to a boil and remove from the heat. Stir in the grilled mangoes and keep warm until ready to serve. Stir well just prior to serving to reincorporate the butter.

PLACE 2 SCOOPS of vanilla ice cream in each bowl and spoon the mango slices and sauce over the ice cream. Place a mint sprig in each bowl and serve immediately.

BEVERAGE SUGGESTION: Rich coffee

BRANDY-MACERATED MISSION FIG ICE CREAM WITH ALMOND TOFFEE

This is a great dessert for the winter months, when many fruits are not readily available. If you don't have an ice-cream maker, the macerated figs can be stirred into slightly softened vanilla ice cream or just spooned over the top.

SERVES 6

1/3 CUP CHOPPED DRIED MISSION FIGS

1/4 CUP BRANDY

3/4 CUP PLUS 3 TABLESPOONS SUGAR

2 CUPS WHIPPING CREAM

1/2 CUP HALF-AND-HALF

1 VANILLA BEAN, SPLIT LENGTHWISE

4 EGG YOLKS

ALMOND TOFFEE (RECIPE FOLLOWS)

PLACE THE FIGS, BRANDY, and 3 tablespoons of the sugar in a small saucepan and bring to a boil. Remove from the heat and refrigerate for 8 hours, or overnight. Strain through a fine-mesh sieve and reserve the figs and sauce separately.

BRING THE CREAM, half-and-half, and vanilla bean to a boil and remove from the heat. Whisk together the remaining 3/4 cup of sugar and the egg yolks. Slowly whisk in some of the hot cream to temper the eggs. Whisk the egg mixture into the cream and cook over low heat for 5 minutes, or until the mixture coats the back of a spoon and steam rises from the top. Strain through a fine-mesh sieve and refrigerate until thoroughly chilled.

POUR THE CUSTARD into an ice-cream maker and spin until frozen. Stir in the figs and freeze until ready to use.

PLACE 2 SCOOPS of the fig ice cream in the center of each bowl. Place a few pieces of the Almond Toffee standing upright in the ice cream and spoon the sauce over the ice cream and around the bowl.

BEVERAGE SUGGESTION: Brandy-coffee drink

Almond Toffee

MAKES ABOUT 2 CUPS

3/4 CUP BUTTER

3/4 CUP BROWN SUGAR

1 CUP DRY-ROASTED WHOLE ALMONDS

1/4 CUP FINELY CHOPPED DRY-ROASTED ALMONDS

6 OUNCES SEMISWEET CHOCOLATE CHIPS

MELT THE BUTTER in a thick-bottomed pot. Stir in the sugar and cook over medium-high heat until the mixture reaches 275° to 280°. Remove from the heat and stir in the whole almonds.

SPRINKLE 2 TABLESPOONS of the chopped almonds on a lightly buttered baking sheet. Pour the sugar mixture onto the baking sheet and spread evenly. Sprinkle the chocolate chips over the toffee and allow them to melt. Spread the melted chocolate evenly over the toffee and dust with the remaining 2 tablespoons of chopped almonds. Refrigerate for 15 minutes, or until cool. Break the Almond Toffee into chunks or cut into uniform shapes. (Extra Almond Toffee can be stored in an airtight container at room temperature for up to 1 week.)

A Trio of Granitas

These light, refreshing granitas are a perfect alternative to sorbet or ice cream. Instead of spinning in an ice-cream machine, they are scraped after freezing to form the light icy texture. Granitas are excellent as a palate cleanser between courses or as a fresh, enticing dessert.

Ironstone Obsession Granita

SERVES 8

2 STALKS LEMONGRASS

1/2 CUP SUGAR

1-INCH PIECE GINGER, SLICED 1/4 INCH THICK

2 CUPS COLD WATER

1/2 CUP IRONSTONE OBSESSION SYMPHONY

1 TABLESPOON FRESHLY SQUEEZED LEMON JUICE

CRUSH THE LEMONGRASS with the side of a knife or the bottom of a skillet. Place in a saucepan with the sugar, ginger, and water. Bring to a boil and simmer for 10 minutes. Remove from the heat and cool. Strain through a fine-mesh sieve and stir in the wine and lemon juice. Pour into a shallow pan and freeze overnight.

SCRAPE THE FROZEN GRANITA with the edge of a spoon to form a light, fluffy ice. Scoop the granita into chilled serving glasses or bowls and serve immediately.

Cabernet Franc–Raspberry Granita

SERVES 8

1 1/2 CUPS WATER

1 CUP CRUSHED RASPBERRIES

1 1/4 CUPS CABERNET FRANC

3/4 CUP SUGAR

COMBINE ALL OF THE INGREDIENTS in a saucepan and bring to a boil. Simmer for 10 minutes and remove from the heat. Cool to room temperature and strain through a fine-mesh sieve. Pour into a shallow pan and freeze overnight.

SCRAPE THE FROZEN GRANITA with the edge of a spoon to form a light, fluffy ice. Scoop the granita into chilled serving glasses or bowls and serve immediately.

WINE SUGGESTION: Obsession, Cabernet Franc, or Shiraz

Shiraz-Plum Granita

SERVES 8

2 CUPS WATER

³/₄ CUP SHIRAZ

³/₄ CUP SUGAR

1 VANILLA BEAN, SPLIT LENGTHWISE

1 CUP PEELED AND CHOPPED PLUMS

COMBINE ALL OF THE INGREDIENTS in a saucepan and bring to a boil. Simmer for 10 minutes and remove from the heat. Cool to room temperature and strain through a fine-mesh sieve. Pour into a shallow pan and freeze overnight.

SCRAPE THE FROZEN GRANITA with the edge of a spoon to form a light, fluffy ice. Scoop the granita into chilled serving glasses or bowls and serve immediately.

AMARETTO-RASPBERRY CRÈME BRÛLÉE

The key to perfect crème brûlée is in the jiggle (that's a technical term). When the crème brûlée first goes in the oven it will slosh (another technical term), not jiggle. About halfway through the cooking time the edges will begin to jiggle, but the center will still slosh. When the center just begins to jiggle, remove it from the oven and let it cool in the water bath and it will be perfect.

SERVES 6

2 CUPS WHIPPING CREAM

5 EGG YOLKS

1/4 CUP PLUS 6 TABLESPOONS SUGAR

2 TABLESPOONS AMARETTO

1/2 CUP RASPBERRIES

BRING THE CREAM to a boil over medium heat. Whisk together the egg yolks and sugar and slowly whisk in some of the hot cream to temper the eggs. Add the egg mixture to the cream and cook for 2 to 3 minutes, or until the mixture coats the back of a spoon and steam rises from the top. Remove from the heat and stir in the amaretto.

PREHEAT THE OVEN to 325°. Place the raspberries in 6 small ovenproof crème brûlée dishes or custard cups and gently ladle in the custard. Place the dishes in a baking pan and add 3/4 inch of hot water to the pan. Bake for 20 to 25 minutes, or until the custard is set. Cool to room temperature and refrigerate for 1 hour, or until thoroughly chilled.

SPRINKLE 1 TABLESPOON of the remaining sugar on each crème brûlée and caramelize with a kitchen torch or under the broiler.

BEVERAGE SUGGESTION: Coffee

MEXICAN CHOCOLATE CUSTARD

Mexican chocolate typically has cinnamon and extra sugar added to it, often to mask the grainy, inferior quality of the chocolate itself. Here, I have mirrored the flavors of the Mexican chocolate, but with the smooth, creamy texture that makes custard one of life's true pleasures.

SERVES 8

2 CUPS SUGAR

1/2 CUP KAHLÚA

1/4 CUP WATER

1/2 CUP TOASTED ALMONDS, FINELY CHOPPED

2 CUPS HALF-AND-HALF

2 CUPS WHIPPING CREAM

7 EGG YOLKS

1/2 TEASPOON GROUND CINNAMON

6 OUNCES CHOPPED BITTERSWEET CHOCOLATE

1 1/2 TABLESPOONS VANILLA EXTRACT

BRING I CUP OF THE SUGAR, the Kahlúa, and water to a boil in a large saucepan over high heat. Lower the heat to medium and simmer for 7 minutes. Remove the syrup from the heat and divide into 8 small ramekins.

PREHEAT THE OVEN TO 300°. Place the almonds, half and half, and cream into the pot from the Kahlúa (don't wash it) and bring to a gentle boil over medium-high heat. Remove from the heat and let stand for 10 minutes.

PLACE THE EGG YOLKS, cinnamon, chocolate, and the remaining 1 cup of sugar in a large mixing bowl. Slowly pour the hot cream into the egg yolk mixture, whisking constantly until all of the chocolate is melted. Add the vanilla extract and strain through a fine-mesh sieve.

LADLE THE CUSTARD into the ramekins and place in a baking pan. Add enough hot water to the pan to come halfway up the sides of the ramekins, and bake for 45 minutes, or until a knife stuck in the center comes out clean. Remove the custards from the oven and cool to room temperature in the water bath. Refrigerate for at least 2 hours, or overnight.

RUN A KNIFE AROUND THE EDGE of the ramekin to loosen the custard. Unmold a custard in the center of each plate, scraping out as much of the Kahlua syrup as possible.

BEVERAGE SUGGESTION: Coffee

RICOTTA OBSESSION

This recipe is where you find out how simple it is to make your own ricotta cheese. Milk, lemon juice, and less than 30 minutes, that's it. Once you try it, you will wonder why you have been paying so much to buy something that is so easy and inexpensive to make.

SERVES 8

1²/₃ CUPS IRONSTONE OBSESSION SYMPHONY

6 THIN SLICES GINGER

¹/₂ CUP SUGAR

2 MANGOES, PEELED AND SLICED ¹/₄ INCH THICK

¹/₂ GALLON WHOLE MILK

¹/₄ CUP FRESHLY SQUEEZED LEMON JUICE

¹/₄ TEASPOON KOSHER SALT

32 WHOLE ALMONDS, TOASTED

8 MINT SPRIGS

BRING THE WINE, ginger, and sugar to a boil in a medium saucepan. Add the mango slices and simmer for 5 minutes, or until the mangoes are tender. Strain the poaching liquid into a small saucepan. Reserve 24 of the mango slices and refrigerate them until ready to use. Remove the ginger slices and discard. Chop the remaining mango pieces and add to the strained poaching liquid. Simmer the liquid for 30 minutes, or until reduced to about 1 cup. Remove the chopped mango and 2 tablespoons of the poaching liquid from the pan and set aside. Simmer the remaining poaching liquid for 15 minutes, or until reduced to about ¹/₂ cup. Refrigerate the resulting glaze until ready to use.

PLACE THE MILK in a thick-bottomed pot and heat to 200°, stirring often so the milk does not scorch. Stir in the lemon juice and return the heat to 200°. Remove the pan from the heat, cover, and let stand for 15 minutes. Line a colander with 5 layers of cheesecloth (or use an aspic strainer) and pour the milk into the colander. Let the curd drain for about 15 minutes (the longer it drains the dryer your cheese will be). Place the curd in a bowl and fold in the kosher salt, chopped mango, and reserved poaching liquid. Cover and refrigerate until thoroughly chilled.

ARRANGE 3 OF THE MANGO SLICES in the center of each plate and top with a scoop of the ricotta cheese. Place 4 almonds on each plate. Drizzle the glaze over the cheese and around the plate and garnish with the mint sprigs.

🍇 WINE SUGGESTION: Semisweet white wine

BREAD PUDDING TRIO

I first experienced the incredible scope of bread pudding when I was living in New Orleans, where they have raised bread pudding to an art form. Every restaurant has their own version and each one seems better than the last. I have included a few of my favorites here, but don't hesitate to branch out into your own favorite flavor combinations.

Strawberry-Vanilla Bread Pudding
SERVES 8

2 CUPS MILK

2 CUPS WHIPPING CREAM

4 EGGS

PINCH OF SALT

1 CUP BROWN SUGAR

1 TEASPOON VANILLA EXTRACT

8 CUPS CUBED DAY-OLD CROISSANTS

12 LARGE STRAWBERRIES, QUARTERED

PREHEAT THE OVEN to 375°. Whisk together the milk, cream, eggs, salt, brown sugar, and vanilla in a large bowl. Add the croissant cubes and stir until completely coated. Let stand for 10 minutes. Fold in the strawberries and spoon into 8 small ovenproof dishes or a 9-inch square baking pan. Bake for 20 to 25 minutes, or until the custard is set.

Cherry-Almond Bread Pudding
SERVES 8

2 CUPS MILK

2 CUPS WHIPPING CREAM

4 EGGS

PINCH OF SALT

1 CUP BROWN SUGAR

1/4 TEASPOON ALMOND EXTRACT

8 CUPS CUBED DAY-OLD SOURDOUGH BREAD, CRUSTS REMOVED

2 CUPS FRESH PITTED BING CHERRIES (OR CANNED IF FRESH ARE NOT AVAILABLE)

PREHEAT THE OVEN to 375°. Whisk together the milk, cream, eggs, salt, brown sugar, and almond extract in a large bowl. Add the bread cubes and stir until completely coated. Let stand for 10 minutes. Add the cherries and spoon into 8 small ovenproof dishes or a 9-inch square baking pan. Bake for 20 to 25 minutes, or until the custard is set.

BEVERAGE SUGGESTION: Cream sherry

Ginger-Pear Bread Pudding

SERVES 8

2 CUPS MILK

2 CUPS WHIPPING CREAM

2-INCH PIECE GINGER, PEELED AND SLICED
   $1/8$ INCH THICK

4 EGGS

PINCH OF SALT

1 CUP SUGAR

8 CUPS CUBED DAY-OLD FRENCH BREAD,
   CRUSTS REMOVED

2 PEARS, PEELED AND CORED

PREHEAT THE OVEN to 375°. Combine the milk, cream, and ginger in a saucepan and bring to a boil. Simmer over low heat for 10 minutes and remove from the heat. Cool to room temperature and strain through a fine-mesh sieve to remove the ginger. Whisk the eggs, salt, and sugar into the cream. Stir in the bread cubes and let stand for 10 minutes. Cut the pears into $1/4$-inch-thick slices about 2 inches long. Add the pears to the pudding and spoon into 8 small ovenproof dishes or a 9-inch square baking pan. Bake for 20 to 25 minutes, or until the custard is set.

CHOCOLATE BREAD PUDDING WITH CARAMEL-PECAN-BOURBON SAUCE

This rich, chocolaty bread pudding is so decadent it will satisfy even the most die-hard chocoholic. Make sure to save any extra Caramel-Pecan-Bourbon Sauce; it is great on brownies, ice cream, cake, or even just with a spoon.

SERVES 9

- 2 CUPS MILK
- 8 OUNCES BITTERSWEET CHOCOLATE, FINELY CHOPPED
- 2 CUPS WHIPPING CREAM
- 6 EGGS
- 1 1/4 CUPS BROWN SUGAR
- 1 1/2 TEASPOONS VANILLA EXTRACT
- PINCH OF SALT
- 6 CUPS DAY-OLD BREAD CUBES
- CARAMEL-PECAN-BOURBON SAUCE (RECIPE FOLLOWS)

PREHEAT THE OVEN TO 350°. Bring the milk to a boil in a medium saucepan over medium-high heat. Remove from the heat, add the chocolate, and stir until melted. Whisk together the cream, eggs, sugar, vanilla, and salt in a large bowl. Slowly whisk in one-third of the chocolate mixture to temper the eggs. Add the remaining chocolate mixture and stir until combined. Add the bread cubes to the bowl and stir until completely coated. Let stand for 10 minutes, or until most of the liquid is absorbed, stirring occasionally.

PLACE THE BREAD MIXTURE in a buttered 9-inch square pan and bake for 1 hour, or until the custard is set. Cool slightly and cut into 3-inch squares.

PLACE A PIECE OF THE WARM BREAD pudding in the center of each plate and top with some of the Caramel-Pecan-Bourbon Sauce.

Caramel-Pecan-Bourbon Sauce
MAKES ABOUT 2 CUPS

- 1 1/4 CUPS SUGAR
- 1/2 CUP WATER
- 1/4 CUP CORN SYRUP
- 1 TABLESPOON FRESHLY SQUEEZED LEMON JUICE
- 1 1/4 CUPS WHIPPING CREAM
- 1 CUP COARSELY CHOPPED TOASTED PECANS
- 2 TABLESPOONS BOURBON

COOK THE SUGAR and water in a heavy-bottomed pan over high heat for 5 minutes, or until the sugar is melted. Add the corn syrup and lemon juice and cook over medium-high heat for 10 minutes, or until amber colored. Add the cream and cook, stirring constantly, until smooth. Remove from the heat and add the pecans and bourbon. Serve warm.

BEVERAGE SUGGESTION: Coffee

FRANGELICO TIRAMISU

This softer, more traditional version of tiramisu is very easy to prepare and will serve a large group. The Frangelico adds a great hazelnut flavor that really sets this tiramisu apart.

5 EGGS, SEPARATED

1/2 CUP SUGAR

2 1/2 POUNDS MASCARPONE CHEESE

1 CUP FRANGELICO

1 1/4 CUPS HALF-AND-HALF

1 CUP BREWED ESPRESSO

90 SMALL LADYFINGER COOKIES

3 TABLESPOONS UNSWEETENED COCOA POWDER

1/2 CUP COARSELY CHOPPED TOASTED HAZELNUTS

BEAT THE EGG YOLKS AND SUGAR until creamy. Add the mascarpone cheese, 1/2 cup of the Frangelico, and the half-and-half and mix until completely combined. Beat the egg whites to soft peaks and fold into the mascarpone mixture.

COMBINE THE ESPRESSO and the remaining 1/2 cup of Frangelico in a measuring cup. Cover the bottom of a 9- by 13-inch pan with a layer of ladyfingers. Drizzle one-third of the espresso mixture over the ladyfingers and dust with one-third of the cocoa. Spread one-third of the mascarpone mixture over the ladyfingers.

REPEAT THE LAYERING PROCESS 2 more times. Place the chopped hazelnuts in a large-holed sieve and dust the top of the tiramisu with the finely chopped nuts, reserving the coarsely ground nuts for garnish. Cover and refrigerate for at least 4 hours.

SCOOP SOME OF THE TIRAMISU onto each plate and sprinkle with the remaining hazelnuts.

BEVERAGE SUGGESTION: Coffee

CABERNET CHOCOLATE TRUFFLES
WITH CABERNET SYRUP

These large, incredibly rich and chocolaty truffles are a luscious ending to any dinner party. The presentation is very impressive, yet they can be completely prepared up to a day in advance. For an extra-special touch, the tops of the truffles can be brushed with edible gold flake.

SERVES 12

2 CUPS CABERNET SAUVIGNON

2 CUPS SUGAR

8 CUPS CHOPPED BITTERSWEET CHOCOLATE

1 1/2 CUPS WHIPPING CREAM

CANDIED ALMOND BRITTLE (RECIPE FOLLOWS)

BRING THE WINE and sugar to boil in a non-reactive saucepan. Simmer over low heat for 1 hour, or until reduced to about 1 1/2 cups. Refrigerate until ready to use.

COMBINE 4 CUPS of the chocolate and the cream in a double boiler and cook over medium heat for 10 minutes, or until the chocolate is completely melted. Stir in 1/4 cup of the Cabernet syrup and refrigerate overnight.

SCOOP THE CHOCOLATE mixture into twelve round golf ball–sized truffles and refrigerate until ready to use.

PLACE THE REMAINING 4 cups of chocolate over a double boiler and stir until smooth. Dip each truffle into the chocolate, evenly coating the entire truffle. Place the dipped truffles on a parchment-lined pan and refrigerate for up to two weeks.

CUT EACH TRUFFLE in half and place 2 halves in the center of each plate. Drizzle some of the remaining Cabernet syrup around the truffle. Using a small paring knife dipped in hot water, carefully melt a slit on one side of the truffle and stand a piece of candied almond in each slit.

Candied Almond Brittle
MAKES ABOUT 2 CUPS

2 CUPS SUGAR

1/2 CUP WATER

1 TABLESPOON LEMON JUICE

1 1/2 CUPS TOASTED, SLICED ALMONDS

COOK THE SUGAR, water, and lemon juice in a large sauté pan over medium-high heat for 10 minutes, or until amber (290° to 295°). Spread the almonds in a thin layer on a lightly greased baking sheet and evenly spread the sugar mixture over the almonds. Let cool and break into approximately 2- by 3-inch pieces.

🍇 WINE SUGGESTION: Cabernet Sauvignon

Menu Ideas

❦

*The following menus are a few
of the combinations of dishes that work
well together. They can be enjoyed
as they are, adjusted to suit your tastes,
or simply used as a guide to prepare
your own menus.*

❧ James Beard House Menu ❧

I have been fortunate to be a guest chef at the James Beard House in New York on two occasions. This compilation of the two dinners showcases foods that are indigenous to California.

HOT SMOKED SALMON IN SAVORY PASTRY CUPS

Ironstone Reserve Chardonnay

• • •

GRILLED DAY BOAT SCALLOPS WITH CUCUMBER
COUSCOUS AND LEMON VINAIGRETTE

Ironstone Sauvignon Blanc

• • •

IRONSTONE OBSESSION GRANITA

• • •

MERLOT-MARINATED GRILLED QUAIL WITH
YUKON GOLD POTATO CAKES

Ironstone Merlot

• • •

MINER'S LETTUCE SALAD WITH
BLACKBERRY-CABERNET VINAIGRETTE

Ironstone Cabernet Sauvignon

• • •

BRANDY-MACERATED MISSION FIG ICE CREAM
WITH ALMOND TOFFEE

Creekside Brandy

❧ SOUTHWESTERN HOLIDAY MENU ❧

*Spice up your holiday meal! This menu contains all of the traditional foods,
but they are prepared in a decidedly untraditional manner.*

CURRIED PUMPKIN SOUP

• • •

PAN SEARED PRAWNS WITH ORANGE-CILANTRO SAUCE

• • •

CHILI-BRINED TURKEY WITH CHORIZO CORNBREAD
STUFFING AND ORANGE-CHILI GLAZE

• • •

OBSESSION SPAGHETTI SQUASH SALAD

• • •

MEXICAN CHOCOLATE CUSTARD

❧ PICNIC MENU ❧

*This is a perfect menu for a relaxing day. All of the dishes can be prepared
at least one day in advance so you can sit by the pool all
day and still serve a delicious meal.*

TUSCAN-STYLE CANNELLI BEANS WITH SAGE

• • •

DAN'S MARINATED MUSSELS

• • •

GAZPACHO SALAD

• • •

ASPARAGUS AND PENNE WITH LEMON CREAM

❧ Red Wine Menu ❧

Here's one for the red wine lovers. All of these dishes pair beautifully with a variety of different red wines, so pull out a couple of your favorites and enjoy.

GRILLED MUSHROOMS WITH CHÈVRE AND GRILLED
TOMATO VINAIGRETTE

• • •

CHICKEN ROULADE WITH WILTED ARUGULA
AND FERMENTED BLACK BEAN DEMI-GLACE

• • •

MINER'S LETTUCE SALAD WITH
BLACKBERRY-CABERNET VINAIGRETTE

• • •

PEPPER-PECAN PORK TENDERLOIN WITH POTATO GRATIN

• • •

CABERNET CHOCOLATE TRUFFLES WITH CABERNET SYRUP

❧ Vineyard Lunch Menu ❧

Here is a luncheon that will impress your guests. All four courses offer big flavor, yet they are still very light. And best of all, they are very easy to prepare.

MISSION FIGS WITH PANCETTA AND BALSAMIC VINEGAR

• • •

NECTARINE AND BUTTER LETTUCE SALAD

• • •

CHICKEN WITH HERBS AND CAPERS

• • •

RICOTTA OBSESSION

❧ Sweetheart Menu ❧

Each of these dishes contains foods that are said to have aphrodisiac effects.
I make no guarantees, but what do you have to lose?
At very least you get a delicious meal!

BARBECUED OYSTERS

• • •

PEPPERED BEEF TENDERLOIN with
DRIED FRUIT–BRANDY SAUCE

• • •

AMARETTO-RASPBERRY CRÈME BRÛLÉE

❧ White Wine Menu ❧

Of course we couldn't forget the white wine lovers. Each of these dishes
has the light fresh flavors that blend so well with white wines.

PEACH-LAVENDER SOUP

• • •

SIX-ONION TARTS with WILD MUSHROOMS and GRUYÈRE

• • •

SOUTHWESTERN CAESAR SALAD

• • •

BARBECUED LOBSTER TAIL with HEARTS of ROMAINE

• • •

RASPBERRY-STUFFED POACHED PEACHES
with OBSESSION SAUCE

Index

Table *of* Equivalents

The exact equivalents in the following tables have been rounded for convenience.

LIQUID AND DRY MEASURES

U.S.	METRIC
$1/2$ teaspoon	2.5 milliliters
1 teaspoon	5 milliliters
1 tablespoon	15 milliliters
1 fluid ounce (2 tablespoons)	30 milliliters
$1/4$ cup	60 milliliters
$1/3$ cup	80 milliliters
$1/2$ cup	120 milliliters
1 cup	240 milliliters
2 cups (1 pint)	475 milliliters
4 cups (1 quart)	950 milliliters
1 gallon (4 quarts)	3.84 liters
1 ounce (by weight)	28 grams
1 pound	454 grams
2.2 pounds	1 kilogram

OVEN TEMPERATURE

FAHRENHEIT	CELSIUS	GAS
250	120	$1/2$
275	135	1
300	150	2
325	165	3
350	180	4
375	190	5
400	205	6
425	220	7
450	230	8
475	245	9
500	260	10

LENGTH

U.S.	METRIC
$1/8$ inch	3 millimeters
$1/4$ inch	6 millimeters
$1/2$ inch	12 millimeters
1 inch	2.5 centimeters

A Kautz Ironstone Vineyards Production
Copyright © 2005 by Kautz Ironstone Vineyards
Photography © 2005 Tim Turner
Recipes © 2005 Dan Lewis

Kautz Ironstone Vineyards
1894 Six Mile Road
Murphys, California 95247
www.ironstonevineyards.com

Photography: Tim Turner
Copyeditor: Judi Carle
Design: Catherine Jacobes Design
Project Editor: Lori Kautz
Text Consultant: Jan Hovey

Set in Requiem, Trade Gothic, Minion and Cezanne.

Library of Congress Cataloging-in-Publication Data
on file with publisher.

ISBN 0-9754924-0-3

Printed in China

First printed in 2005.

1 2 3 4 5 6 7 8 9 10 — 09 08 07 06 05